BOOKS AND BOOKMEN

BOOKS AND BOOKMEN
AND OTHER ESSAYS

By
JOHN WATSON, *1850 -1907*
(IAN MACLAREN, pseud.)

Essay Index Reprint Series

BOOKS FOR LIBRARIES PRESS
FREEPORT, NEW YORK

First Published 1912
Reprinted 1971

INTERNATIONAL STANDARD BOOK NUMBER:
0-8369-2083-X

LIBRARY OF CONGRESS CATALOG CARD NUMBER:
72-142709

PRINTED IN THE UNITED STATES OF AMERICA

CONTENTS

BOOKS AND BOOKMEN

Books and Bookmen

THEY cannot be separated any more than sheep and a shepherd, but I am minded to speak of the bookman rather than of his books, and so it will be best at the outset to define the tribe.

It does not follow that one is a bookman because he has many books, for he may be a book huckster or his books may be those without which a gentleman's library is not complete. And in the present imperfect arrangement of life one may be a bookman and yet have very few books, since he has not the wherewithal to purchase them. It is the foolishness of his kind to desire a loved author in some becoming dress, and his fastidiousness to ignore a friend in a four-pence-halfpenny edition. The bookman, like the poet, and a good many other people, is born and not made, and my grateful memory retains an illustration of the difference between a bookowner and a bookman which I think is apropos. As he was to preside at a lecture I

was delivering he had in his courtesy invited
me to dinner, which was excellent, and as he
proposed to take the rôle that night of a man
who had been successful in business, but yet
allowed himself in leisure moments to trifle
with literature, he desired to create an atmosphere, and so he proposed with a certain im-
posing air that we should visit what he called
" my library." Across the magnificence of
the hall we went in stately procession, he first,
with that kind of walk by which a surveyor of
taxes could have at once assessed his income,
and I, the humblest of the bookman tribe, following in the rear, trembling like a skiff in
the wake of an ocean liner. " There," he
said, with his thumbs in the armholes of his
waistcoat, " what do you think of that? "
And *that* was without question a very large
and ornate and costly mahogany bookcase
with glass doors. Before I saw the doors I
had no doubt about my host, but they were a
seal upon my faith, for although a bookman
is obliged to have one bit of glass in his garden for certain rare plants from Russia and
Morocco, to say nothing of the gold and white
vellum lily upon which the air must not be
allowed to blow, especially when charged

with gas and rich in dust, yet he hates this conservatory, just as much as he loves its contents.   His contentment is to have the flowers laid out in open beds, where he can pluck a blossom at will.   As often as one sees the books behind doors, and most of all when the doors are locked, then he knows that the owner is not their lover, who keeps tryst with them in the evening hours when the work of the day is done, but their jailer, who has bought them in the market-place for gold, and holds them in this foreign place by force. It has seemed to me as if certain old friends looked out from their prison with appealing glance, and one has been tempted to break the glass and let, for instance, Elia go free.   It would be like the emancipation of a slave. Elia was not, good luck for him, within this particular prison, and I was brought back from every temptation to break the laws of property by my chairman, who was still pursuing his catechism.   "What," was question two, " do you think I paid for *that?* "   It was a hopeless catechism, for I had never possessed anything like *that,* and none of my friends had in their homes anything like *that,* and in my wildest moments I had never asked

the price of such a thing as *that*. As it
loomed up before me in its speckless respectability and insolence of solid wealth my English sense of reverence for money awoke, and
I confessed that this matter was too high for
me; but even then, casting a glance of depre-
cation in its direction, I noticed *that* was almost filled by a single work, and I wondered
what it could be. "Cost £80 if it cost a
penny, and I bought it second-hand in perfect
condition for £17, 5s., with the books thrown
in — *All the Year Round* from the beginning
in half calf;" and then we returned in procession to the drawing-room, where my pa-
tron apologised for our absence, and explained that when two bookmen got together
over books it was difficult to tear them away.
He was an admirable chairman, for he occu-
pied no time with a review of literature in *his*
address, and he slept without being noticed
through mine (which is all I ask of a chairman), and so it may seem ungrateful, but in
spite of " *that* " and any books, even Spenser
and Chaucer, which *that* might have con-
tained, this Mæcenas of an evening was not a
bookman.

It is said, and now I am going to turn the

application of a pleasant anecdote upside down, that a Colonial squatter having made his pile and bethinking himself of his soul, wrote home to an old friend to send him out some chests of books, as many as he thought fit, and the best that he could find. His friend was so touched by this sign of grace that he spent a month of love over the commission, and was vastly pleased when he sent off, in the best editions and in pleasant binding, the very essence of English literature. It was a disappointment that the only acknowledgment of his trouble came on a postcard, to say that the consignment had arrived in good condition. A year afterwards, so runs the story, he received a letter which was brief and to the point. "Have been working over the books, and if anything new has been written by William Shakespeare or John Milton, please send it out." I believe this is mentioned as an instance of barbarism. It cannot be denied that it showed a certain ignorance of the history of literature, which might be excused in a bushman, but it also proved, which is much more important, that he had the smack of letters in him, for being turned loose without the guide of any training in this wide field, he

fixed as by instinct on the two classics of the
English tongue. With the help of all our
education, and all our reviews, could you and
I have done better, and are we not every day,
in our approval of unworthy books, doing
very much worse. Quiet men coming home
from business and reading, for the sixth time,
some noble English classic, would smile in
their modesty if any one should call them
bookmen, but in so doing they have a sounder
judgment in literature than coteries of clever
people who go crazy for a brief time over the
tweetling of a minor poet, or the preciosity
of some fantastic critic.

There are those who buy their right to citi-
zenship in the commonwealth of bookmen,
but this bushman was free-born, and the sign
of the free-born is, that without critics to aid
him, or the training of a University, he knows
the difference between books which are so
much printed stuff and a good book which is
" the Precious life-blood of a Master Spirit."
The bookman will of course upon occasion
trifle with various kinds of reading, and there
is one member of the brotherhood who has a
devouring thirst for detective stories, and has
always been very grateful to the creator of

Sherlock Holmes.   It is the merest pedantry
for a man to defend himself with a shamed
face for his light reading: it is enough that
he should be able to distinguish between the
books which come and go and those which
remain.   So far as I remember, *The Mystery
of a Hansom Cab* and *John Inglesant* came
out somewhat about the same time, and there
were those of us who read them both; but
while we thought the *Hansom Cab* a very in-
genious plot which helped us to forget the tedium of a railway journey, I do not know that
there is a copy on our shelves.   Certainly it
is not lying between *The Ordeal of Richard
Feverel* and *The Mayor of Casterbridge.*
But some of us venture to think that in that
admirable historical romance which moves
with such firm foot through both the troubled
England and the mysterious Italy of the
seventeenth century, Mr. Shorthouse won a
certain place in English literature.

When people are raving between the soup
and fish about some popular novel which to-
morrow will be forgotten, but which doubtless, like the moths which make beautiful the
summer-time, has its purpose in the world of
speech, it gives one bookman whom I know

the keenest pleasure to ask his fair companion whether she has read *Mark Rutherford.* He is proudly conscious at the time that he is a witness to perfection in a gay world which is content with excitement, and he would be more than human if he had not in him a touch of the literary Pharisee. She has *not* read *Mark Rutherford,* and he does not advise her to seek it at the circulating library, because it will not be there, and if she got it she would never read more than ten pages. Twenty thousand people will greedily read *Twice Murdered and Once Hung* and no doubt they have their reward, while only twenty people read *Mark Rutherford;* but then the multitude do not read *Twice Murdered* twice, while the twenty turn again and again to Mark for its strong thinking and its pure sinewy English style. And the children of the twenty thousand will not know *Twice Murdered,* but the children of the twenty, with others added to them, will know and love *Mark Rutherford.* Mr. Augustine Birrell makes it, I think, a point of friendship that a man should love George Borrow, whom I think to appreciate is an excellent but an acquired taste; there are others who would propose *Mark Rutherford* and the *Revelation in Tanner's Lane* as a sound test for a bookman's palate. But . . . de gustibus . . . !

It is the chief office of the critic, while encouraging all honest work which either can instruct or amuse, to distinguish between the books which must be content to pass and the books which must remain because they have an immortality of necessity. According to the weightiest of French critics of our time the author of such a book is one " who has enriched the human mind, who has really added to its treasures, who has got it to take a step further . . . who has spoken to all in a style of his own, yet a style which finds itself the style of everybody, in a style that is at once new and antique, and is the contemporary of all the ages." Without doubt Sainte-Beuve has here touched the classical quality in literature as with a needle, for that book is a classic to be placed beside Homer and Virgil and Dante and Shakespeare — among the immortals — which has wisdom which we cannot find elsewhere, and whose form has risen above the limitation of any single age. While ordinary books are houses which serve for a generation or two at most, this kind of book

is the Cathedral which towers above the
building at its base and can be seen from afar,
in which many generations shall find their
peace and inspiration. While other books are
like the humble craft which ply from place to
place along the coast, this book is as a stately
merchantman which compasses the great
waters and returns with a golden argosy.

The subject of the book does not enter into
the matter, and on subjects the bookman is
very catholic, and has an orthodox horror of
all sects. He does not require Mr. Froude's
delightful apology to win the *Pilgrim's Progress* a place on his shelf, because, although the
bookman may be far removed from Puritan-
ism, yet he knows that Bunyan had the secret
of English style, and although he may be as
far from Romanism, yet he must needs have
his A'Kempis, especially in Pickering's edition of 1828, and when he places the two
books side by side in the department of religion, he has a standing regret that there is no
Pilgrim's Progress also in Pickering.

Without a complete Milton he could not be
content. He would like to have Masson's life
too in 6 vols. (with index), and he is apt to
consider the great Puritan's prose still finer

than his poetry, and will often take down the Areopagitica that he may breathe the air of high latitudes; but he has a corner in his heart for that evil living and mendacious bravo but most perfect artist, Benvenuto Cellini. While he counts Gibbon's, I mean Smith and Milman's Gibbon's Rome in 8 vols., blue cloth, the very model of histories, yet he revels in those books which are the material for historians, the scattered stones out of which he builds his house, such as the diaries of John Evelyn and our gossip Pepys, and that scandalous book, *Grammont's Memoirs,* and that most credulous but interesting of Scots annalists, Robert Wodrow.

According to the bookman, but not, I am sorry to say, in popular judgment, the most toothsome kind of literature is the Essay, and you will find close to his hand a dainty volume of Lamb open perhaps at that charming paper on " Imperfect Sympathies," and though the bookman be a Scot yet his palate is pleasantly tickled by Lamb's description of his national character — Lamb and the Scots did not agree through an incompatibility of humour — and near by he keeps his Hazlitt, whom he sometimes considers the most virile writer of the century: nor would he be quite happy unless he could find in the dark *The Autocrat of the Breakfast Table.* He is much indebted to a London publisher for a very careful edition of the *Spectator,* and still more to that good bookman, Mr. Austin Dobson, for his admirable introduction. As the bookman's father was also a bookman, for the blessing descendeth unto the third and fourth generation, he was early taught to love De Quincey, and although, being a truthful man, he cannot swear he has read every page in all the fifteen volumes — roxburghe calf — yet he knows his way about in that whimsical, discursive, but ever satisfying writer, who will write on anything, or any person, always with freshness and in good English, from the character of Judas Iscariot and " Murder as a Fine Art " to the Lake Poets — there never was a Lake school — and the Essenes. He has much to say on Homer, and a good deal also on " Flogging in Schools "; he can hardly let go Immanuel Kant, but if he does it is to give his views, which are not favourable, of *Wilhelm Meister;* he is not above considering the art of cooking potatoes or the question of whether human beings once had tails, and in his theological moods he will expound St. John's Epistles, or the principles of Christianity. The bookman, in fact, is a quite illogical and irresponsible being, who dare not claim that he searches for accurate information in his books as for fine gold, and he has been known to say that that department of books of various kinds which come under the head of " what's what," and " why's why," and " where's where," are not literature. He does not care, and that may be foolish, whether he agrees with the writer, and there are times when he does not inquire too curiously whether the writer be respectable, which is very wrong, but he is pleased if this man who died a year ago or three hundred years has seen something with his own eyes and can tell him what he saw in words that still have in them the breath of life, and he will go with cheerful inconsequence from Chaucer, the jolliest of all book companions, and Rabelais — although that brilliant satirist had pages which the bookman avoids, because they make his gorge rise — to Don Quixote. If he carries a Horace, Pickering's little gem, in his waistcoat pocket, and sometimes pictures that genial Roman club-man in the Savile, he has

none the less an appetite for Marcus Aurelius.
The bookman has a series of love affairs before he is captured and settles down, say, with
his favourite novel, and even after he is a mid-
dle-aged married man he must confess to one
or two book friendships which are perilous to
his inflammable heart.

In the days of calf love every boy has first
tasted the sweetness of literature in two of
the best novels ever written, as well as two of
the best pieces of good English.   One is *Rob-
inson Crusoe* and the other the *Pilgrim's
Progress*.   Both were written by masters of
our tongue, and they remain until this day
the purest and most appetising introduction
to the book passion.   They created two
worlds of adventure with minute vivid de-
tails and constant surprises — the foot on the
sand, for instance, in *Crusoe,* and the valley
of the shadow with the hobgoblin in *Pilgrim's
Progress* — and one will have a tenderness
for these two first loves even until the end.
Afterwards one went afield and sometimes got
into queer company, not bad but simply a little common.   There was an endless series of
Red Indian stories in my school-days, wherein
trappers could track the enemy by a broken

blade of grass, and the enemy escaped by coming down the river under a log, and the price was sixpence each. We used to pass the tuck-shop at school for three days on end in order that we might possess *Leaping Deer, the Shawnee Spy*. We toadied shamefully to the owner of *Bull's Eye Joe,* who, we understood, had been the sole protection of a frontier state. Again and again have I tried to find one of those early friends, and in many places have I inquired, but my humble companions have disappeared and left no signs, like country children one played with in holiday times.

It appears, however, that I have not been the only lover of the trapper stories, nor the only one who has missed his friends, for I received a letter not long ago from a bookman telling me that he had seen my complaint somewhere, and sending me the *Frontier Angel* on loan strictly that I might have an hour's sinless enjoyment. He also said he was on the track of *Bill Bidden,* another famous trapper, and hoped to send me word that Bill was found, whose original value was sixpence, but for whom this bookman was now prepared to pay gold. One, of course, does not mean that the Indian and trapper stories had the same claim to be literature as the *Pilgrim's Progress,* for, be it said with reverence, there was not much distinction in the style, or art in the narrative, but they were romances, and their subjects suited boys, who are barbarians, and there are moments when we are barbarians again, and above all things these tales bring back the days of long ago.   It was later that one fell under the power of two more mature and exacting charmers, Mayne Reid's *Rifle Rangers* and Dumas' *Monte Cristo.* The *Rangers* has vanished with many another possession of the past, but I still retain in a grateful memory the scene where Rube, the Indian fighter, who is supposed to have perished in a prairie fire and is being mourned by the hero, emerges with much humour from the inside of a buffalo which was lying dead upon the plain, and rails at the idea that he could be wiped out so easily. Whether imagination has been at work or not I do not know, but that is how my memory has it now, and to this day I count that resurrection a piece of most fetching work.

Rambling through a bookshop a few months ago I lighted on a copy of *Monte*

Cristo and bought it greedily, for there was a railway journey before me. It is a critical experiment to meet a love of early days after the years have come and gone. This stout and very conventional woman — the mother of thirteen children — could she have been the black-eyed, slim girl to whom you and a dozen other lads lost their hearts? On the whole, one would rather have cherished the former portrait and not have seen the original in her last estate. It was therefore with a flutter of delight that one found in this case the old charm as fresh as ever — meaning, of course, the prison escape with its amazing ingenuity and breathless interest.

When one had lost his bashfulness and could associate with grown-up books, then he was admitted to the company of Scott, and Thackeray, and Dickens, who were and are, as far as one can see, to be the leaders of society. My fond recollection goes back to an evening in the early sixties when a father read to his boy the first three chapters of the *Pickwick Papers* from the green-coloured parts, and it is a bitter regret that in some clearance of books that precious *Pickwick* was allowed to go, as is supposed, with a lot of pamphlets on Church and State, to the great gain of an unscrupulous dealer.

The editions of Scott are now innumerable, each more tempting than the other; but affection turns back to the old red and white, in forty-eight volumes, wherein one first fell under the magician's spell. Thackeray, for some reason I cannot recall, unless it were a prejudice in our home, I did not read in youth, but since then I have never escaped from the fascination of *Vanity Fair* and *The Newcomes,* and another about which I am to speak. What giants there were in the old days, when an average Englishman, tried by some business worry, would say, " Never mind, Thackeray's new book will be out to-morrow." They stand, these three sets, Scott, Thackeray, and Dickens, the very heart of one's library of fiction. Wearied by sex novels, problem novels, theological novels, and all the other novels with a purpose, one returns to the shelf and takes down a volume from this circle, not because one has not read it, but because one has read it thirty times and wishes for sheer pleasure's sake to read it again. Just as a tired man throws off his dress coat and slips on an old study jacket, so one lays down the latest thoughtful or intense or something worse pseudo work of fiction, and is at ease with an old gossip who is ever wise and cheery, who never preaches and yet gives one a fillip of goodness. Among the masters one must give a foremost place to Balzac, who strikes one as the master of the art in French literature. It is amazing that in his own day he was not appreciated at his full value, and that it was really left to time to discover and vindicate his position. He is the true founder of the realistic school in everything wherein that school deserves respect, and has been loyal to art. He is also certain to maintain his hold and be an example to writers after many modern realists have been utterly and justly forgotten.

Two books from the shelf of fiction are taken down and read once a year by a certain bookman from beginning to end, and in this matter he is now in the position of a Mohammedan converted to Christianity who is advised by the missionary to choose one of his two wives to have and to hold as a lawful spouse. When one has given his heart to *Henry Esmond* and the *Heart of Midlothian* he is in a strait, and begins to doubt the ex-

pediency of literary monogamy. Of course,
if it go by technique and finish, then *Esmond*
has it, which from first to last in conception
and execution is an altogether lovely book;
and if it go by heroes — Esmond and Butler
— then again there is no comparison, for the
grandson of Cromwell's trooper was a very
wearisome, pedantic, grey-coloured Puritan
in whom one cannot affect the slightest interest. How poorly he compares with Henry
Esmond, who was slow and diffident, but a
very brave, chivalrous, single-hearted, modest
gentleman, such as Thackeray loved to describe. Were it not heresy to our Lady Castlewood, whom all must love and serve, it also
comes to one that Henry and Beatrix would
have made a complete pair if she had put
some assurance in him and he had instilled
some principle into her, and Henry Esmond
might have married his young kinswoman had
he been more masterful and self-confident.
Thackeray takes us to a larger and gayer scene
than Scott's Edinburgh of narrow streets and
gloomy jails and working people and old
world theology, but yet it may be after all
Scott is stronger. No bit of history, for instance, in *Esmond* takes such a grip of the im-

agination as the story of the Porteous mob.
After a single reading one carries that night
scene etched for ever in his memory.   The
sullen, ruthless crowd of dour Scots, the grey
rugged houses lit up by the glare of the
torches, the irresistible storming of the Tol-
booth, the abject helplessness of Porteous in
the hands of his enemies, the austere and judicial self-restraint of the people, who did
their work as those who were serving justice,
their care to provide a minister for the crimi-
nal's last devotions, and their quiet dispersal
after the execution — all this remains unto
this day the most powerful description of
lynch law in fiction.   The very strength of
old Edinburgh and of the Scots-folk is in the
Heart of Midlothian.   The rivalry, however,
between these two books must be decided by
the heroine, and it seems dangerous to the
lover of Scott to let Thackeray's fine lady
stand side by side with our plain peasant girl,
yet soul for soul which was greater, Rachel of
Castlewood or Jeanie Deans?   Lady Castlewood must be taken at the chief moment in
Esmond, when she says to Esmond: " To-day,
Henry, in the anthem when they sang, ' When
the Lord turned the captivity of Zion we were

like them that dream '— I thought, yes, like
them that dream, and then it went, ' They that
sow in tears shall reap in joy; and he that
goeth forth and weepeth, shall doubtless come
again with rejoicing, bringing his sheaves
with him.' I looked up from the book and
saw you; I was not surprised when I saw
you, I knew you would come, my dear,
and I saw the gold sunshine round your head."

That she said as she laughed and sobbed,
crying out wildly, " Bringing your sheaves
with you, your sheaves with you." And this
again, as Esmond thinks of her, is surely
beaten gold. " Gracious God, who was he,
weak and friendless creature, that such a love
should be poured out upon him; not in vain,
not in vain has he lived that such a treasure
be given him? What is ambition compared
to that but selfish vanity? To be rich, to be
famous: what do these profit a year hence
when other names sound louder than yours,
when you lie hidden away under the ground
along with the idle titles engraven on your
coffin? Only true love lives after you, follows your memory with secret blessing or pre-
cedes you and intercedes for you. ' Non om-
nis moriar '— if dying I yet live in a tender

heart or two, nor am lost and hopeless living, if a sainted departed soul still loves and prays for me." This seems to me the second finest passage in English fiction, and the finest is when Jeanie Deans went to London and pleaded with the Queen for the life of her condemned sister, for is there any plea in all literature so eloquent in pathos and so true to human nature as this, when the Scottish peasant girl poured forth her heart: " When the hour of trouble comes to the mind or to the body — and seldom may it visit your ladyship — and when the hour of death that comes to high and low — lang and late may it be yours — oh, my lady, then it is na' what we hae dune for oursels but what we hae dune for ithers that we think on maist pleasantly. And the thought that ye hae intervened to spare the puir thing's life will be sweeter in that hour, come when it may, than if a word of your mouth could hang the haill Porteous mob at the tail of ae tow." Jeanie Deans is the strongest woman in the gallery of Scott, and an embodiment of all that is sober, and strong, and conscientious, and passionate in Scotch nature.

The bookman has indeed no trouble arranging his gossips in his mind, where they hold good fellowship, but he is careful to keep them apart upon his bookshelves, and when he comes home after an absence and finds his study has been tidied, which in the feminine mind means putting things in order, and to the bookman general anarchy (it was the real reason Eve was put out of Eden), when he comes home, I say, and finds that happy but indecorous rascal Boccaccio, holding his very sides for laughter, between Lecky's *History of European Morals* and Law's *Serious Call,* both admirable books, then the bookman is much exhilarated. Because of the mischief that is in him he will not relieve those two excellent men of that disgraceful Italian's company for a little space, but if he finds that the domestic sprite has thrust a Puritan between two Anglican theologians he effects a separation without delay, for a religious controversy with its din and clatter is more than he can bear.

The bookman is indeed perpetually engaged in his form of spring cleaning, which is rearranging his books, and is always hoping to square the circle, in both collecting the books of one department together, and also having his books in equal sizes. After a brief glance at a folio and an octavo side by side he gives up that attempt, but although he may have to be content to see his large Augustine, Benedictine edition, in the same row with Bayle's Dictionary, he does not like it and comforts himself by thrusting in between, as a kind of mediator, Spotswood's *History of the Church of Scotland* with *Burnett's Memoirs of the Dukes of Hamilton,* that edition which has the rare portrait of Charles I. by Faithorne. He will be all his life rearranging, and so comes to understand how it is that women spend forenoons of delight in box rooms or store closets, and are happiest when everything is turned upside down. It is a slow business, rearrangement, for one cannot flit a book bound after the taste of Grolier, with graceful interlacement and wealth of small ornaments, without going to the window and lingering for a moment over the glorious art, and one cannot handle a *Compleat Angler* without tasting again some favourite passage. It is days before five shelves are reconstructed, days of unmixed delight, a perpetual whirl of gaiety, as if one had been at a conversazione, where all kinds of famous people whom you had known afar had been gathered together and you had spoken to each as if he had been the friend of your boyhood. It is in fact a time of reminiscences, when the two of you, the other being Sir Thomas Browne, or Goldsmith, or Scott, or Thackeray, go over passages together which contain the sweetest recollections of the past. When the bookman reads the various suggestions for a holiday which are encouraged in the daily newspapers for commercial purposes about the month of July, he is vastly amused by their futility, and often thinks of pointing out the only holiday which is perfectly satisfying. It is to have a week without letters and without visitors, with no work to do, and no hours, either for rising up or lying down, and to spend the week in a library, his own, of course, by preference, opening out by a level window into an old-fashioned garden where the roses are in full bloom, and to wander as he pleases from flower to flower where the spirit of the books and the fragrance of the roses mingle in one delight.

Times there are when he would like to hold a meeting of bookmen, each of whom should be a mighty hunter, and he would dare to invite Cosmo Medici, who was as keen about books as he was about commerce, and according to Gibbon used to import Indian spices and Greek books by the same vessel, and that admirable Bishop of Durham who was as joyful on reaching Paris as the Jewish pilgrim was when he went to Sion, because of the books that were there. " O Blessed God of Gods, what a rush of the glow of Pleasure rejoiced our hearts, as often as we visited Paris, the Paradise of the World! There we long to remain, where on account of the greatness of our love the days ever appear to us to be few. There are delightful libraries in cells redolent with aromatics, there flourishing greenhouses of all sorts of volumes, there academic meads, trembling with the earthquake of Athenian Peripatetics pacing up and down, there the promontory of Parnassus and the Porticoes of the Stoics." The Duke of Roxburghe and Earl Spencer, two gallant sportsmen whose spoils have enriched the land; Monkbarns also, though we will not let him bring any antiquities with him, jagged or otherwise; and Charles Lamb, whom we shall coax into telling over again how he started out at ten o'clock on Saturday night and

roused up old Barker in Covent Garden, and
came home in triumph with " that folio Beau-
mont and Fletcher," going forth almost in
tears lest the book should be gone, and coming
home rejoicing, carrying his sheaf with him.
Besides, whether Bodley and Dibdin like it
or not, we must have a Royalty, for there were
Queens who collected, and also on occasions
stole books, and though she be not the greatest of the Queenly bookwomen and did not
steal, we shall invite Mary Queen of Scots,
while she is living in Holyrood, and has her
library beside her. Mary had a fine collection of books well chosen and beautifully
bound, and as I look now at the catalogue it
seems to me a library more learned than is
likely to be found even in the study of an ad-
vanced young woman of to-day. A Book of
Devotion which was said to have belonged to
her and afterwards to a Pope, gloriously
bound, I was once allowed to look upon, but
did not buy, because the price was marked in
plain figures at a thousand guineas. It would
be something to sit in a corner and hear Monkbarns and Charles Lamb comparing notes,
and to watch for the moment when Lamb
would withdraw all he had said against the

Scots people, or Earl Spencer describing with delight to the Duke of Roxburghe the battle of the Sale. But I will guarantee that the whole company of bookworms would end in paying tribute to that intelligent and very fascinating young woman from Holyrood, who still turns men's heads across the stretch of centuries. For even a bookman has got a heart.

Like most diseases the mania for books is hereditary, and if the father is touched with it the son can hardly escape, and it is not even necessary that the son should have known his father. For Sainte-Beuve's father died when he was an infant and his mother had no book tastes, but his father left him his books with many comments on the margins, and the book microbe was conveyed by the pages. " I was born," said the great critic in the *Consolations,* " I was born in a time of mourning; my cradle rested on a coffin . . . my father left me his soul, mind, and taste written on every margin of his books." When a boy grows up beside his father and his father is in the last stages of the book disease, there is hardly any power which can save that son, unless the mother be robustly illiterate, in which case the crossing of the blood may make him impervious. For a father of this kind will unconsciously inoculate his boy, allowing him to play beside him in the bookroom, where the air is charged with germs (against which there is no disinfectant, I believe, except commercial conversation), and when the child is weary of his toys will give him an old book of travels, with quaint pictures which never depart from the memory. By and by, so thoughtless is this invalid father, who has suffered enough, surely, himself from this disease, that he will allow his boy to open parcels of books, reeking with infection, and explain to him the rarity of a certain first edition, or show him the thickness of the paper and the glory of the black-letter in an ancient book. Afterwards, when the boy himself has taken ill and begun on his own account to prowl through the smaller bookstalls, his father will listen greedily to the stories he has to tell in the evening, and will chuckle aloud when one day the poor victim of this deadly illness comes home with a newspaper of the time of Charles II., which he has bought for threepence. It is only a question of time when that lad, being now on an allowance of his own,

will be going about in a suit of disgracefully
shabby tweeds, that he may purchase a The-
ophrastus of fine print and binding upon
which he has long had his eye, and will be
taking milk and bread for his lunch in the
city, because he has a foolish ambition to ac-
quire by a year's saving the Kelmscott edition
of the *Golden Legend.* A change of air
might cure him, as for instance twenty years'
residence on an American ranch, but even then
on his return the disease might break out
again: indeed the chances are strong that he
is really incurable. Last week I saw such a
case — the bookman of the second generation
in a certain shop where such unfortunates col-
lect. For an hour he had been there browsing
along the shelves, his hat tilted back upon his
head that he might hold the books the nearer
to his eyes, and an umbrella under his left
arm, projecting awkwardly, which he had not
laid down, because he did not intend to stay
more than two minutes, and knew indeed, as
the father of a family, that he ought not to be
there at all. He often drops in, for this is
not one of those stores where a tradesman hur-
ries forward to ask what you want and offers
you the last novel which has captivated the

juicy British palate; the bookman regards
such a place with the same feeling that a phy-
sician has to a patent drug store. The dealer
in this place so loved his books that he almost
preferred a customer who knew them above
one who bought them, and honestly felt a pang
when a choice book was sold. Never can I
forget what the great Quaritch said to me
when he was showing me the inner shrine of
his treasure-house, and I felt it honest to explain that I could only look, lest he should
think me an impostor. "I would sooner
show such books to a man that loved them
though he couldn't buy them, than a man who
gave me my price and didn't know what he
had got." With this slight anecdote I would
in passing pay the tribute of bookmen to the
chief hunter of big game in our day.

When the bookman is a family man, and I
have sometimes doubts whether he ought not
to be a celibate like missionaries of religion
and other persons called to special devotion,
he has of course to battle against his temptation, and his struggles are very pathetic. The
parallel between dipsomania and bibliomania
is very close and suggestive, and I have often
thought that more should be made of it. It

is the wife who in both cases is usually the sufferer and good angel, and under her happy influence the bookman will sometimes take the pledge, and for him, it is needless to say, there is only one cure. He cannot be a moderate drinker, for there is no possibility of moderation, and if he is to be saved he must become a total abstainer. He must sign the pledge, and the pledge must be made of a solemn character with witnesses, say his poor afflicted wife and some intelligent self-made Philistine. Perhaps it might run like this: " I, A. B., do hereby promise that I will never buy a classical book in any tongue, or any book in a rare edition; that I will never spend money on books in tree-calf or tooled morocco; that I shall never enter a real old bookshop, but should it be necessary shall purchase my books at a dry goods store, and there shall never buy anything but the cheapest religious literature, or occasionally a popular story for my wife, and to this promise I solemnly set my hand." With the ruin of his family before his eyes, or at least, let us say, the disgraceful condition of the dining-room carpet, he intends to keep his word, and for a whole fortnight will not allow himself to en-

ter the street of his favourite bookshop.
Next week, however, business, so he says at
least, takes him down the street, but he remembers the danger, and makes a brave effort
to pass a public-house. The mischief of the
thing, however, is that there is another public-
house in the street and passing it whets the la-
tent appetite, and when he is making a brave
dash past his own, some poor inebriate, coming out reluctantly, holds the door open, and
the smell is too much for his new-born virtue.
He will go in just for a moment to pass the
time of day with his friend the publican and
see his last brand of books, but not to buy —
I mean to drink — and then he comes across
a little volume, the smallest and slimmest of
volumes, a mere trifle of a thing, and not dear,
but a thing which does not often turn up, and
which would just round off his collection at
a particular point. It is only a mere taste,
not downright drinking; but ah me, it sets him
on fire again, and I who had seen him go in
and then by a providence have met his wife
coming out from buying that carpet, told her
where her husband was, and saw her go to
fetch him. Among the touching incidents of
life, none comes nearer me than to see the

bookman's wife pleading with him to remember his (once) prosperous home and his (almost) starving children.   And indeed if there be any other as entirely affecting in this province, it is the triumphant cunning with which the bookman will smuggle a suspicious brown paper parcel into his study at an hour when his wife is out, or the effrontery with which he will declare, when caught, that the books have been sent unbeknown to him, and he supposes merely for his examination.   For, like drink, this fearsome disease eats into the very fibre of character, so that its victim will practise tricks to obtain books in advance of a rival collector, and will tell the most mendacious stories about what he paid for them.

Should he desire a book, and it be not a king's ransom, there is no sacrifice he will not make to obtain it.   His modest glass of Burgundy he will cheerfully give up, and if he ever travelled by any higher class, which is not likely, he will now go third, and his topcoat he will make last another year, and I do not say he will not smoke, but a cigar will now leave him unmoved.   Yes, and if he gets a chance to do an extra piece of writing, between 12 and 2 A. M., he will clutch at the opportunity, and all that he saves, he will calculate shilling by shilling, and the book he purchases with the complete price — that is the price to which he has brought down the seller after two days' negotiations — anxious yet joyful days — will be all the dearer to him for his self-denial. He has also anodynes for his conscience when he seems to be wronging his afflicted family, for is he not gathering the best of legacies for his sons, something which will make their houses rich for ever, or if things come to the worst cannot his collecion be sold and all he has expended be restored with usury, which in passing I may say is a vain dream. But at any rate, if other men spend money on dinners and on sport, and carved furniture and gay clothing, may he not also have one luxury in life? His conscience, however, does give painful twinges, and he will leave the Pines Horace which he has been handling delicately for three weeks, in hopeless admiration of its marvellous typography, and be outside the door before a happy thought strikes him, and he returns to buy it, after thirty minutes' bargaining, with perfect confidence and a sense of personal generosity. What gave him this relief and now suffuses his very soul with charity? It was a date which for the moment he had forgotten and which has occurred most fortunately. To-morrow will be the birthday of a man whom he has known all his days and more intimately than any other person, and although he has not so high an idea of the man as the world is good enough to hold, and although he has often quarrelled with him and called him shocking names — which tomcats would be ashamed of — yet he has at the bottom a sneaking fondness for the fellow, and some-times hopes he is not quite so bad after all. One thing is certain, the rascal loves a good book and likes to have it when he can, and per-haps it will make him a better man to show that he has been remembered and that one per-son at least believes in him, and so the book-man orders that delightful treasure to be sent to his own address in order that next day he may present it — as a birthday present — to himself.

Concerning tastes in pleasure there can be no final judgment, but for the bookman it may be said, beyond any other sportsman, he has the most constant satisfaction, for to him there is no close season, except the spring cleaning which he furiously resents, and only allows one in five years, and his autumn holiday, but then he takes some six handy volumes with him. For him there are no hindrances of weather, for if the day be sunshine he taketh his pleasure in a garden, and if the day be sleet of March the fireside is the dearer, and there is a certain volume — Payne's binding, red morocco, which was a favourite colour of Payne's — and the bookman reads *Don Quixote* with the more relish because the snow-drift is beating on the window. During the hours of the day when he is visiting patients, who tell their symptoms at intolerable length, or dictating letters about corn, or composing sermons, which will not always run, the bookman is thinking of the quiet hour which will lengthen into one hundred and eighty minutes, when he shall have his reward, the kindliest for which a man can work or hope to get. He will spend the time in the good company of people who will not quarrel with him, nor will he quarrel with them. Some of them of high estate and some extremely low; some of them learned persons and some of them simple, country men. For while the bookman counteth it his chief hon-

our and singular privilege to hold converse
with Virgil and Dante, with Shakespeare and
Bacon, and such-like nobility, yet is he very
happy with Bailie Nicol Jarvie and Dandie
Dinmont, with Mr. Micawber and Mrs.
Gamp; he is proud when Diana Vernon
comes to his room, and he has a chair for
Colonel Newcome; he likes to hear Coleridge
preach, who, as Lamb said, "never did anything else," and is much flattered when
Browning tries to explain what he meant in
Paracelsus. It repays one for much worry
when William Blake not only reads his *Songs
of Innocence* but also shows his own illustration, and he turns to his life of Michael
Angelo with the better understanding after he
has read what Michael Angelo wrote to Vit-
toria Colonna. He that hath such friends,
grave or gay, needeth not to care whether he
be rich or poor, whether he know great folk
or they pass him by, for he is independent of
society and all its whims, and almost independent of circumstances. His friends of
this circle will never play him false nor ever
take the pet. If he does not wish their company they are silent, and then when he turns
to them again there is no difference in the wel-

come, for they maintain an equal mind and
are ever in good humour. As he comes in
tired and possibly upset by smaller people
they receive him in a kindly fashion, and in
the firelight their familiar faces make his
heart glad. Once I stood in Emerson's room,
and I saw the last words that he wrote, the
pad on which he wrote them, and the pen with
which they were written, and the words are
these: "The Book is a sure friend, always
ready at your first leisure, opens to the very
page you desire, and shuts at your first fa-
tigue."

As the bookman grows old and many of his
pleasures cease, he thanks God for one which
grows the richer for the years and never fades.
He pities those who have not this retreat from
the weariness of life, nor this quiet place in
which to sit when the sun is setting. By the
mellow wisdom of his books and the immortal
hope of the greater writers he is kept from
peevishness and discontent, from bigotry and
despair. Certain books grow dearer to him
with the years, so that their pages are worn
brown and thin, and he hopes with a Birming-
ham book-lover, Dr. Showell Rogers, whose
dream has been fulfilled, that Heaven, having

a place for each true man, may be " a bookman's paradise, where early black-lettered
tomes, rare and stately, first folios of Shakespeare, tall copies of the right editions of the
Elzevirs, and vellumed volumes galore, un-
cropped, uncut, and unfoxed in all their ver-
dant pureness, fresh as when they left the
presses of the Aldi, are to be had for the asking." Between this man at least and his books
there will be no separation this side the grave,
but his gratitude to them and his devotion
will ever grow and their ministries to him be
ever dearer, especially that Book of books
which has been the surest guide of the human
soul. "While I live," says one who both
wrote and loved books and was one of our
finest critics, " while I live and think, nothing
can deprive me of my value for such treasures.
I can help the appreciation of them while I
last and love them till I die, and perhaps if
fortune turns her face once more in kindness
upon me before I go, I may chance, some
quiet day, to lay my overbeating temples on
a book, and so have the death I most envy."

HUMOUR: AN ANALYSIS

HUMOUR: AN ANALYSIS

AS a writer on any subject is apt to have a partial mind, I desire to clear myself at once from all prejudice by offering to my judicial readers the assurance of my profound conviction that a sense of humour is a hindrance to practical success in life, but of course they will notice the qualified form of my statement. To have an eye for the recurring comedy of things, so that no absurdity of speech or incident escapes, is a joy to the individual, sustaining him wonderfully amid the labours and stupidities of life, and very likely it is also a joy to his friends, who have learned from him to use the wholesome medicine of laughter. But if you come to one's daily calling and make the two exceptions of literature and caricature in Art, who has not suffered through the affliction of humour? If the humorist, and I am not now speaking of a merely jocose person, but of one who has a real palate for comedy, happens to be a clergyman, then he runs the greatest risk in his as-

sociation with good people, for with a few exceptions, which are only tolerated and apologised for, this class will say things in all seriousness which such a man will not be able to
resist, and one brief break-down may ruin his
character for life. He will be afraid to attend a religious meeting, lest some worthy
speaker, having raised his audience to the
highest pitch of pious expectation, should top-
ple over into an anti-climax; and funerals
will be to him a double trial, because comedy
lies so near to tragedy. It gets upon this poor
man's nerves when a neighbour whom he has
seen coming along the street, round-faced and
chirpy, enters the room with an expression of
dolorous woe, shakes hands with the under-
taker instead of the chief mourner, and is
heard to remark with much unction and a sigh
which stirs the atmosphere, " There to-day
and here to-morrow, much missed." One unhappy clergyman still blushes with shame as
he recalls an incident of his early days when,
in a northern city, he was sent to take a funeral
service in the kitchen of a workingman's
house. They sat round him, eight Scots ar-
tisans, each in his Sunday blacks, with his pipe
projecting from his waistcoat pocket, and his

hat below his chair, looking with awful, immovable countenance into the eternities. It seemed irreverent to speak to any one of the graven images, but the poor minister required to know something about the man who had died, and so he ventured to ask the figure next him in a whisper what the deceased had been? Whereupon the figure answered with a loud, clear voice, " I dinna ken myself, for I jest came here wi' a friend," and then, addressing a still more awful figure opposite, and in a still more aggressive tone, " Jeems, what was the corpse to a trade? " After which the trembling minister wished he had left the matter alone.

Will a medical man be acceptable to that large class of patients who love to speak of their ailments and have nothing wrong with them, if they discover that he is laughing at them, and especially if he allows himself the relief of sarcasm? Is it not better for his income, if not for his science, that he should be able to listen with a murmur of sympathy to old ladies of both sexes describing their symptoms, and prescribe the most harmless of mixtures with an owl-like countenance, beseeching them not to lose heart, even in such desperate

circumstances, and departing with the assurance that he is at their service night and day,
and must be sent for instantly if the coloured
water gives no relief?   They say two Roman
Augurs could not look at one another without
laughing, but how much more ought to be
pitied the consultant and the general practi-
tioner who meet over the case of a hypochon-
driac?

I challenge any one to mention a politician
of our time who, on the whole, has not lost,
rather than gained, through humour; and I
fancy no man should be more afraid of this
tricky gift than a leader of the democracy.
Had Mr. Gladstone possessed the faintest
sense of the ridiculous amid the multitude of
his rich and brilliant talents, he had not been
able to address a crowd from the window of
his railway carriage, and receive a gift of a
plaid, or a walking-stick, or, if my memory
does not fail me, a case of marmalade, until
his outraged fellow-passengers, anxious to
make connections, insisted the train should go
on, and it departed to the accompaniment of
the statesman's eloquent peroration.   But it
was just because Mr. Gladstone could do such
things, and was always in the most deadly

earnest, that the people trusted him and hung upon his words. Nothing was so dangerous a snare to Lord Beaconsfield as his abounding and delightful humour, for it lodged in the minds of the English people a suspicion which never departed, that that brilliant man, who had been so farseeing in his ideas and anticipations of the trend of events, was little else than a charlatan and a scorner; and I fancy that Lord Salisbury's most devoted followers would have been glad if some of his mordant jests had never passed beyond his study. Is there not another most accomplished and attractive personality in politics who has forfeited the chance of supreme authority, partly no doubt by a pronounced individualism, but partly also by a graceful lightness of touch and allusion which are not judged consistent with that fierce sincerity which has been the strength of his party? Toleration is never without a flavour of humour, but humour is an absolute disability to fanaticism. With this genial sense of humanity no man can be a fanatic, and in a recent book on French crime it is frequently mentioned that the principal miscreants were intense persons with no humour, so that in this branch of life, quite as much as in politics, the humorous person is severely handicapped. One feels as if his money and his life were safe in the hands of a person who can enjoy an honest jest, but this may only prove that the person is lacking in that determination and enterprise which are conditions of practical success in a strenuous modern community.

So far as a layman in such affairs can judge, humour is alien to the business mind, and would forfeit any character for stability. The looker-on, who, of course, may be a very foolish person, is amazed at the substantial success of dull men and the respect in which they are held, and he is equally amazed at the suspicion with which bright men, whose conversation sparkles and enlivens, are regarded and the slight esteem in which they are held. The former may be wooden to the last point of exasperation, but his neighbours pronounce him to be solid, and thrust him into directorships, chairmanships, the magistracy and Parliament, and after a long course of solidity and success, with increasing woodenness, he will likely reach the House of Lords. But the other man, with whom you spent so pleasant an evening, and who is as much at home

among books as " a stable-boy among horses,"
is apt to be judged light metal — a person
who may know his Shakespeare, but could not
be trusted with things of value like money.
There are times when one loses heart and almost concludes that the condition of tangible
success in English life is to be well-built, giv-
ing a pledge to fortune in a moderate stout-
ness, to have a solemn expression of face, sug-
gesting the possession of more wisdom than is
likely to have been given to any single person,
to be able to hold one's tongue till some in-
cautious talker has afforded an idea, and to
have the gift of oracular commonplace.   If
to such rare talents can be added an im-
pressive clearance of the throat, there are few
positions in Church or State, short of the highest, to which their owner may not climb.   My
advice, therefore, to younger men, if indeed
I am expected to give advice to anybody, is to
congratulate themselves that by the will of
Providence they have been cleansed from this
dangerous quality, or, if this be not their for-
tunate case, to hide the possession of humour
behind a mask of sustained impenetrable common sense.

Having made this explanation, to protect

both my subject and myself, I come to the
analysis of humour and would remind you of
its immense variety. It was, I think, George
Eliot who said that nothing was a more serious cause of diversion than incompatibility in
humour, and this observation may also remind
us that we ought to be most catholic in our
judgment of humour. It is fair to argue that
the complexion of humour in different coun-
tries can be referred, like many other things,
to the climate, and it were unfair to expect
the same quality from a Scot, brought up under the grey skies and keen east wind and austere buildings of Edinburgh, as from a
Frenchman, nurtured amid the brightness and
gaiety of Paris, where the spirit of France is
at its keenest if not its strongest. If one desired to pluck the finest flower of humour —
the rare and delicate orchid of this garden —
I mean wit, he must go to France and French
letters. In the French novelists and journal-
ists, but especially in the essayists, whether
he desire its more caustic form in Pascal, or
prefer it lighter and more cynical in Rochefoucauld, one learns how swift and subtle,
how finished and penetrating is the spirit of

wit. Matthew Arnold, perhaps through his devotion to French literature, and Mr. Birrell through his native genius, proved that wit has not been unknown in the English essays, that fine form of literature whose decay always means the decay of culture; and Charles Lamb was often so happy in his wit (it came more nearly sometimes to the English fun), and knew how dangerous it was to have a humorous reputation, that he used to say, " Hush! look solemn. A fool is coming."

But it may be frankly admitted that wit is not acclimatised in England, and that its flavour is not often tasted in English literature; for instance, the following conversation would hardly have been possible in London. Two men were driving along a Boulevard of Paris in an open carriage: one, the host, a successful and sensible person, and the other light and clever; and the conversation of the millionaire grew so ponderous that the other could endure it no longer. He laid his hand upon his host's arm and with the other pointed to a man standing under a tree and just within the furthest range of human vision. The man was yawning, not with the restraint of polite society, but with the open enjoyment of our canine friends. "Look!" said the bright man, in his despair, "and I pray you silence. We are already overheard." This seems to my poor judgment so perfect an instance of wit that I do not supplement it from literature, though I do not offer it for indiscriminate use. It is indeed a story which divides the sheep from the goats, and you must take care to whom you tell it. Once, in magnifying the *esprit* of the French, I offered this to a lady at dinner as an illustration, and she promptly replied, "If that be all you can say for French wit, I do not see much in it." I was desolated not to have had the approval of her taste, and ventured to ask wherein my poor story had failed. "Well, for one thing," this excellent lady, full of common sense and good works, replied, "How could the man hear at that distance?" Then, as Matthew Arnold said about Benjamin Franklin, one knew the limits of triumphant common sense, and as I had been taught in the days of long ago never to put any lady to confusion, it only remained to confess that I had never thought of that, and to thank her for her correction. But I was fully aware that she would only be the more firmly convinced that the French people and myself were condemned in one abyss of stupidity.

If, however, wit be one of the few unconsidered trifles which the English people have not picked up in their world mission of civilisation, we may congratulate ourselves upon the loss, for no humour is more futile and more dangerous for practical purposes. Wit is the inhabitant of clubs and literary *salons;* it is the child of cloistered culture, not of the stirring market-place. Pity the candidate for public suffrages who should employ this tricky weapon. Suppose he give his best point the keen edge of wit, it will doubtless touch a handful in the crowd, and they will flash back a quick response to him, but the other ninety-nine per cent. who have felt nothing will conclude there is a conspiracy between him and a few superior people to insult them and shut them out, and they will regard the speaker with silent resentment, as one who has spoken in cypher to a few. You need not expect any man's vote or any man's favour if you have innocently suggested that he is a fool and beneath your notice. And I dare to say that nothing is more unpopular, as nothing is

more undemocratic, than wit, which is the
aristocracy of humour.   The most democratic
form of humour, and by that I mean the form
which affects the largest number of people in
the shortest space of time and carries them the
farthest distance, is the characteristic humour
of England which we call by the old-fashioned
name of fun.   Fun has no marked intellectual quality, and makes no demand upon the
hearer save that he be not cynical or misan-
thropical.   It is a sense of the obvious comedy of life, its glaring contrasts, its patent ab-
surdities, its ridiculous mistakes, its mirth-
provoking situations.   It is the humour of the
public schools, of the railway carriage, of the
market-place, and of the playroom.   It is like
the air-bells which dance upon the surface of
the water and relieve the blackness beneath.
With a touch of fun a speaker can win his
audience to his side, a master can sweeten his
relations with his workmen, a clever person
who could make good fun might even stop a
riot; and where there is fun a father and his
sons are bound to get on together.   Fun has
lent a certain geniality and jolliness to English life, and it has saved public life from that
rancorous bitterness which, as Mr. Bodley

points out in his admirable *France,* disfigures
French politics. Had there been more honest and wholesome fun in the North, Scottish
life, both in the home and in the Church,
would not have been so grave and contro-
versial. This popular humour in its play on
words has its best exponents in Sydney Smith
and Tom Hood. When one recalls how
Smith told the little girl that she might as
well pat the roof of St. Paul's Cathedral in
order to please the Dean and Chapter as
stroke the shell of a tortoise in order to please
it, and how Hood was given a wine-glass of
ink instead of his black draught, and promptly
offered to swallow a piece of blotting-paper
as an antidote, one is simply selecting at
random from the bag two specimens of good
English fooling. The *Pickwick Papers* afford a very carnival of rollicking humour in
incident, and with their plea for charity have
done more than a multitude of sermons to
cheer and sweeten English life. Whatever
may be said by superior persons who always
apologise for laughing, it is a good thing that
the people should be moved from time to time
to pure and kindly laughter, and when a mob
laughs after the English fashion the police

may be withdrawn, and when a nation takes
to laughing at folly, then folly, whether intellectual or moral, has lost half its danger.
In Art one has pleasure in citing our admirable *Punch,* which through a long career has
sustained an honourable tradition of purity
and dignity, and I dare to say we ought to be
thankful for the service our caricaturists have
rendered to the amenities both of public and
private life. Our English humour may be
simple, as a Frenchman or an American allows himself to suggest, but it has its own ad-
vantage. If one compares *Punch* with the
daring illustrated papers of Paris, he will
have a fresh appreciation of purity, and be
thankful that what we laugh at in England
can be laid upon our family table. And if he
compares Mr. Punch with the exceedingly
clever caricaturists of America, he will have
a new idea of English good-nature, and be
thankful for artists who still believe in the romance of marriage and the beauty of simple
emotions. No one, for instance, can examine
the work of Dana Gibson, the American
" black and white " artist, without being impressed both by its intellectual subtlety and
by its artistic finish. But he must also be de-

pressed by the constant suggestion of the weakness, the sordidness, the hypocrisy, and the hopelessness of human society. French and American caricatures tend to lower one's temperature, but English caricature in its master hands tends to raise one's heart, and to inspire one with faith in his fellow-creatures. English humour may prick delusions, but it spares us our dreams; it may play round a wilful peculiarity, it never jeers at an irreparable calamity; it may exhibit the foibles of humanity, it has a tear ready for its sorrows. It is the humour of a people which has not yet lost faith in God and man, which is not yet convinced that the law of life is a nervous scramble for gold; it is a humour which can give a hard blow, but always with the fist and never with a stiletto, and forgets the fight the moment it is over. Long may it flourish in English life and English homes, a check on absurdity of every kind, a cure for melancholy, an incentive to humanity.

The Duke of Wellington was a good John Bull in all his ways, and had his hours when he enjoyed a bit of fun and found it not unuseful. Louis Philippe introduced one of the Marshals of the Peninsular War to our Iron

Duke. They had met before but not in Courts, and the Marshal, with a keen recollection of his experiences at the hands of the Duke, forgot the perfect manners of his people and his own generosity. He refused, it is said, to shake hands with his former opponent, and even allowed himself to turn his back and to walk towards the door. The King apologised profusely to the Duke for the Marshal's discourtesy, but the Duke only laughed with a big, hearty English laugh, and, looking at the Marshal's retreating figure with keen delight, said to His Majesty, " Forgive him, Sire. I taught him that lesson! "

When one passes from England to Ireland, he finds himself in a country which has bred a humour of its own — a plant which cannot be grown in any other soil, and whose very origin cannot be traced. Nothing can be found on the face of the earth so captivating and irresistible, so unexpected and unreasonable, as Irish drollery. It seems as if Nature, in creating that charming people, had invested them with all kinds of bewitching qualities, and then had been pleased, by way of a merry jest and that the world might not grow too solemn, to have inverted the Irish intellect so that it stands upon its head and not upon its feet, which, of course, is the cause of bulls and all the other quips and cranks of the Irish spirit. If any one is still young enough to stand upon his head in his familiar room, he will get a view of the place perfectly novel and surprising, different from anything he could have seen when standing on his feet, and the account he will give of that room will startle every person by its originality. In like fashion it has been given to the Irish mind to have an outlook on life absolutely its own, to go into Wonderland with Alice, and to live in a topsy-turvy world where in truth, to quote an older classic, " the dish runs off with the spoon, and the cow jumps over the moon." If the just and honourable, but perhaps also over-sensible and somewhat phlegmatic persons, who have in recent times had charge of Irish affairs, and have been trying to unravel the tangled skein, had appreciated the tricky sprite which inhabits the Irish mind, and had made a little more allowance for people who are not moved by argument and the multiplication table, but are touched by sentiment and romance as well as vastly tickled by the absurdity of things, they might have achieved greater success, and done more good to a chivalrous, unworldly, quick-witted, and warm-hearted people.

Lever, beloved by schoolboys in past days and by many other people, admirably represents in fiction this gay, incalculable, irresponsible humour (who has not rejoiced in Micky Free?), and he is also supported by many a short story teller, such as the author of *Father Tom and the Pope,* which appeared in *Maga* in the days when the Blackwood circle was the admiration of the land.   Some pessimists fear that the excessive devotion of the Irish people to politics in recent days, who are as delightfully illogical there as in other departments, has had a depressing effect upon their minds, and that we need no longer expect the springs of Irish humour to make green the wilderness.   But this is taking too dark a view of affairs.   The Irish priest and the Irish resident magistrate, and sometimes even the tourist in Ireland, is still refreshed from time to time, and goes on his way rejoicing. It is not so long ago that an Irish peasant dreamt he was visiting the late Queen Victoria, and was asked by the Queen what he would like to drink. When he expressed the humble wish for a glass of the liquor associated with the name of Jamieson, and when the Queen, still full of hospitality, wanted to know whether he would take it hot or cold, he was foolish enough to prefer it hot. As the kettle was not boiling, Her Majesty in the dream hastened to make up the fire with her own hands, while her thirsty and loyal Irish subject waited anxiously. Alas! when the water came to the boil, the noise of the steam awoke him. " Holy St. Patrick!" he said, with infinite regret, " I'll take it cold next time." So far as I know, the Irishman is still living who was sent by his master with a present of a live hare to a neighbour. The hare escaped and the servant made no effort to pursue it, but that was not for the reason which would have affected a Scotsman, that he could not have caught it, but for another reason which could only have occurred to the Irish mind, but to that mind was absolutely satisfactory: " Ye may run and run and run, ye deludhering baste, but it's no use, for ye haven't got the address."

Various pleasant tales have been going round about that genial Irish Judge who died

a few years ago, and whose death diminishes
the gaiety of at least one nation, but I have
not seen it mentioned how he explained the
working of a new Act which lowered the
qualification for Grand Jurymen. "I will
tell you," he said, in his charming brogue,
"what happened at the first Assize I took
afterwards. I gave my usual charge to the
Grand Jury, and I said, 'Gentlemen, you will
be pleased to take your accustomed place in
the Court,' and I give you my word for it, ten
of them went instantly into the dock." Nor
am I sure any one has placed on record a play
on words which it were an insult to call a
"pun," and which crosses the border of the
brightest wit. A man was tried for an
agrarian murder and witnesses swore that they
had seen him commit it, and there was, in fact,
no doubt of his guilt; but the jury promptly
brought him in "Not Guilty." Whereupon
the counsel for the prosecution asked the
judge whether such a verdict could be law.
"I am not prepared," said the judge, "to call
it law, but I am sure it is jurisprudence."
And it is only an Irish Member of Parliament who could congratulate an honourable
baronet, who had bored the House with an

interminable harangue, upon three things. First, " upon speaking so long without stopping "; second, " upon speaking so long without saying anything "; and thirdly, " upon sitting down on his own hat without his head being in it."

It is natural to cross from Ireland to America, but it is not easy to estimate the humour of our kinsmen, because, although we know what it has been, we are not sure what it is going to be. If environment gives the complexion to thought, then one understands why the American jests should be on a large scale, ranging from Artemus Ward, who did so much to delight us all and died in early manhood, to Mark Twain, who lived to complete a task of the highest honour. But it is a question whether the permanent humour of that bright people, whose brain as much as their atmosphere seems charged with electricity will not approximate in the end to the Sa Atticum of France, as their women's talk and dresses remind one of Paris. Any one who reads *Life,* I mean the American *Punch,* can recall a dozen instances of wit as finished, as caustic and, I regret to say, sometimes as profane as any in French modern letters. It

seems as if American humour were between
the tides with the old school of the *Bigelow
Papers* and the *Innocents Abroad* closing its
happy career and the new school hardly yet
in evidence.   American humour at least illus-
trates one characteristic of this hustling modern time; it is suggestive rather than exhaus-
tive, and never can be anticipated.   Our
fathers not only endured but welcomed stories
the end of which they could see from the beginning; they honoured every intermediate
station with a preparatory laugh, and when
the train finally entered the terminus fell almost into an apoplexy, and then, when they
had recovered, were willing, and almost expected that the train should be taken out and
make another entry, or perhaps two, and in
every case it would be received with fresh ap-
probation.   This obvious jocosity is now intolerable; the modern demands brevity and
surprise, that stories should, in fact, be con-
structed with a certain amount of art.   The
modern indeed believes that while Nature in
the shape of an incident belongs to all, its artistic representation in the shape of a picture
is copyright, and that if a man has worked on
a story without which it is indeed not worth

hearing, he ought to be protected in his rights. An old scholar whom I know holds that there are only ten stories, and have only been ten in human history, and that they can all be found as protoplasm in the Greek comedians, and that all the other stories are only evolutions, skilful cross-breedings or adaptations to environment. Nothing, at any rate, is more interesting from a technical point of view than to see how a master in the craft will clothe the barest skeleton of fact with flesh and blood, or how, to vary the situation, he will take an old house that has fallen into disrepair, and, by throwing out a window here and a wing there, by re-facing and re-painting and very often, in the case of old stories, attending carefully to the sanitation (which was very bad in some stories of the past), will astonish us with a new house. The Americans are masters in the art of construction, and provided you are not in the secret it would be a very shrewd person who could tell where the story is to land him.

As, for instance, a lawyer is briefed to defend a man charged with murder and discovers that his client's case is almost hopeless. Anxious to do his best, however, he interviews a genial Irishman who follows the calling of a professional juryman, and pledges him to be on duty when this case is tried. " And remember," said the lawyer, " whatever the other jurymen want, you bring in a verdict of manslaughter." Next day the evidence is even worse than could have been imagined, and the jury are so long in coming back the lawyer is afraid that justice has miscarried. But at last they return with the arranged verdict of manslaughter. When the lawyer called in the evening to recompense his ally, he asked him what in the world had kept the jury so long. " I never was shut up with eleven such obstinate men in my life " (a very ancient jest, mark you, introduced merely as a foil) —" I never was shut up with eleven such obstinate men in my life. They were going to bring in the prisoner ' Not Guilty.' "

Before identifying the humour of the Scot, which is a province by itself with a clearly-marked frontier, it must be remembered that there are two distinct races within the nation of Scotland, and that although they have come under the conformity of one land and largely of one creed, yet the Scots Highlander and the Scots Lowlander are quite opposite types;

they share neither their virtues nor their vices. The Lowlander, the man of Fifeshire or of Ayrshire, is self-controlled, far-seeing, persevering, industrious, with a genius for the accumulation of money. He fulfils the conditions of success in the modern world, and like "jingling Geordie" in the *Fortunes of Nigel,* who was the pioneer of his race in successful emigration, he gathers money wherever he goes, and would make a fortune on a desert island. But our Highlander is impulsive, imaginative, gallant to a fault, and regardless of consequences, pure in life, courteous in manner, chivalrous in ideals. He was at home in the world which is dying, and made the best of raiders and fighting soldiers, as he was the most loyal of clansmen and the child of lost causes, dwelling amid his mountains and by the side of sea lochs in a country of mists and weird, lonely moors, dominated for centuries by a severe and unbending creed. Fun and wit were impossible for him, and yet under his sombre countenance struggled something of the ineradicable humour of the Celt. His humour, so far as it can be defined, is a kind of solemn and long drawn-out waggery which he tastes without a smile, and

of which one would suppose that he is sometimes unconscious.

"Who had this place last year?" asked a
shooting tenant of his keeper.

"Well," said Donald, "I'm not denying
that he wass an Englishman, and he wass a
good man, oh yes, and went to kirk and shot
fery well. But he wass narrow, fery narrow."

"Narrow," said the tenant in amazement,
for the charge was generally the other way
about. "What was he narrow in?"

"Well," said Donald, "I will be telling
you, and it wass this way. The twelfth wass
a fery good day and we had fifty-two brace,
but it wass warm, oh yes, fery warm, and
when we came back to the lodge the gentleman will say to me, 'It iss warm,' and I will
not be contradicting him. Then he will be
saying, 'You will be thirsty, Donald,' and I
will not be contradicting him. Then he will
take out his flask and be speaking about a
dram, and I will not be contradicting him but
will just say, 'Toots, toots.' And then when
the glass wass half full I will say, just for po-
liteness, 'Stop,' *and he stopped*. Oh yes, a
fery narrow man!" In fact, as Donald sug-

gested, a mere literalist, held in the bondage of the letter and without the liberty of the spirit.

Another tenant was making arrangements for the coming winter before he went South, and told the keeper to get the woman who had looked after the lodge the previous winter to take charge of it again.

" You will be meaning Janet Cameron, but I am not advising you to have Janet this year. Oh, no! it will maybe be better not to have Janet this winter."

" Why, what was wrong with her? " and then, with that painful suspicion of the Highlander which greatly hurts his feelings, " Did she drink? "

" Janet," replied Donald with severity, " iss not the woman to be tasting. Oh, no! she iss a good-living woman, Janet, and has the true doctrine, but I will not be saying that you should have her."

" I see. So you and she, I suppose, quarrel? "

" It iss not this man who will be quarrelling with Janet Cameron, who iss his wife's cousin four times removed, and a fery good woman, though she be a Cameron."

"Well, ask her to take the lodge, and offer her the same wages as last year, and a little more, if that will please her, and tell me what she says."

"It iss not for wages Janet Cameron will work; oh, no! that iss not the kind of woman Janet iss, and it iss no use asking her, for she will not come."

"Well," said the Englishman, getting nettled, "do as you are bid and give her the chance, at any rate, and tell me what she says."

"No, sir, it will be wasting my time going, and I will not be asking her." Then, after a pause, "Ye would maybe not be knowin' that Janet iss dead?"

Does any one say with impatience, why did he not tell that at once? If you can answer that question you can lay bare the secret of the Celtic mind, which is the most complex thing in psychology. An Englishman's idea of conversation is a straight line, the shortest distance between two points, but a Celt's idea is a circle, a roundabout way of reaching the same place. He has so long been stalking deer, and other people, that the habit has passed into his mind, and conversation becomes a prolonged stalk in which he is con-

sidering the wind and the colour of the hill-
sides, and avails himself of every bush, and
then comes suddenly upon his prey. His
mind is so subtle that he dislikes statements
of downright brutality and prefers to suggest
rather than assert, and the following is surely
a guarded delicacy of suggestion:

"Why, Hamish," said the Laird to a young
fellow whom he met on the road, "what are
you doing here?   Have you left the situation
I got for you?"

"It is a great sorrow, sir, to this man, but I
could not be staying in that place, and so I
have just come back, and maybe I will be getting something else to do."

"Look here, I don't understand this," said
the Laird.   "Was the work too heavy, or did
they not pay you enough wages?   Tell me
what ailed you at the place."

"I would be ashamed to complain of work,
and there was nothing wrong with the wages;
but it was just this way, and though I'm making no complaint, maybe you will be understanding.   There was a sheep died on the hill
of its own accord, and the master had it salted
and we ate that sheep.   By-and-by there was
a cow died suddenly, and we did not know

what was wrong with her, but the master had
that cow salted and we ate her.   And then the
master's mother took ill, and we were feeling
very anxious, for we will not be forgetting the
sheep and the cow.   And the master's mother
died, and I left."

Upon the English habit of a straight question and a straight answer in the briefest form
of words, you can get no information in the
Highlands.   If, for instance, you desired to
know whether the minister of a parish were
a man of high character and good preaching
gift, you would have to introduce your in-
quiry after a long conversation on things in
general, and then to mix it up with a multitude of detail, and when the other man had
replied the words he used would in themselves
be quite useless for quotation, but you would
have found out his mind.   One of our most
distinguished Highland ministers, who understood his race through and through, desired
to know whether a certain candidate for a
parish had approved himself to the people
and was likely to be appointed.   He called
upon one of the religious worthies of the dis-
trict, being perfectly certain that if he found
out his private opinion he would know the

position. Duncan knew quite well why the
minister had come, and the minister knew that
Duncan knew, but they talked on the weather
and the crop, and the last heresy case, and the
spread of false doctrine in the Lowlands, for
half-an-hour. After that they came as it
were by accident on the name of the candidate,
and Duncan simply covered him with praise.
The minister knew that that counted for nothing. A little later the minister said to Duncan, " I would like to have your mind about
that young man "— his mind, you notice, being very different from his speech. Then
Duncan delivered himself as follows:

" Yesterday I wass sitting on the bank of the
river, and I wass meditating, when a little boy
came and began to fish. He wass a pretty
boy, and I am judging wass fery well brought
up. He talked fery nicely to me, and had the
good manners. He had a fery nice little rod
in his hand, and he did not fling his line badly.
It wass fery pleasant to watch him. But it
wass a great peety that he had forgot to put
a hook on the end of the line, for I did not
notice that he caught many fish, but he wass
a fery nice boy, and I liked him fery much.
And it iss a great mercy that we are getting

good weather for the harvest, for we are not worthy of such goodness, with all our sins and backslidings."

Then the minister knew that that candidate would not get the parish, but Duncan was entitled to say that he had never mentioned the candidate's name, or said a single word against him.

It may seem, perhaps, that the range of humour in its various kinds is exhausted, and that no distinctive form is left for Scotland; in which case it would be the first time that Scotland has not had her share in the division of spoil.   As a matter of fact, there is one humour that has not been touched, which may not be the brightest, nor the subtlest, nor the kindliest, but which is the strongest and most telling of all.   It is that humour which came to a height in Old Testament Scripture, when a Hebrew prophet set himself down to the elaborate, merciless, unanswerable mockery of idolatry.   When he describes the idolater, resolving to add a new god to the furniture of his house, and anxious, like an economical man, that this new piece of furniture should be an heirloom to his children, choosing a tree that will not rot, making a contract with a

clever artisan in the god-making trades, and
then dropping in to see the progress of his
work, watching the wood measured off, the
workmen resting after their labour on the
hard material, the finishing of the thing, and
then the inaugural feast when he worships the
god that has been made out of a log, and cooks
the feast with the shavings which are over, so
that one part of the tree gives him his god and
the other his dinner.   It is a humour which
scorches like flaming fire and bites like vitriol.
And to this humour the Scot has been heir
in modern literature and life.   The Satires of
Horace and even of Juvenal pale before the
unlicensed ridicule of Sir David Lindsay of
the Mount before the Reformation, and one
cannot mention a history seasoned with such
contemptuous mockery as Knox's famous *History of the Reformation in Scotland*.   Burns's
Holy Willie and Carlyle's *Latter-day Pamphlets* show how permanent and how virile is
this spirit of hot indignation and sombre sarcasm in the genius of the Scots people.

It has been difficult for a Scot to forgive the
good-natured and superficial English humorist who not only denied to the Northern
folk any sense of humour, but enshrined his

charge in a too memorable surgical illustration; but the Scot is much comforted with the
reflection that if he has not always arisen to
the play of simple jocosity or the jingle of a
pun, this has only been that he preferred humour of a severer and intellectual kind. The
Scots are a serious people, with an admirable
gravity of mind and a keen literary conscience, and their nature does not allow them
to take humour so lightly and irresponsibly as
their Southern neighbours. If a jest calls at
an English door, and especially if he be
dressed with an obvious simplicity, then it re-
ceives a ready welcome, and if the walls of the
house be also extremely Southern the people
next door will know their neighbour has been
amused, and next day the worthy man will be
introducing his jest in public conveyances,
and even impressing it upon friends with his
thumb. It is impossible not to admire this
childlike simplicity of nature, this willingness
to be amused on easy terms, but it is not the
blame of the Scot that his brain is somewhat
more complicated and that his demands are
more exacting. When a jest calls at a Scot's
door, he is inclined to look out at the upper
window and to inquire if it be a jest at all; but

if he is finally convinced that it is no pre-
tender, which may not be for four-and-twenty
hours of careful examination, none will give
the visitor more hearty welcome. Even then
he may not laugh, but may indeed look more
serious than before; but surely, if there be a
sorrow too deep for tears, there may be a humour too high for laughter, and in the very
earnestness of the Scot's face under the enjoyment of a joke you have a proof of the sincerity of his tribute to humour.

If fun be a sense of the delightful comedy
of things, irony, the humour of the Scots, is
a sense of the underlying tragedy of things, of
the contradictions and mysteries of life, which
have in them a sad absurdity. It is the sport
of the immortals. From this irony he never
quite escapes, and his humour therefore can
never have the gay abandonment and rollicking exuberance of Southern people, but will
always be somewhat austere and restrained,
and move in the shadow rather than in the
light. The helplessness of men in the hands
of Almighty and inscrutable powers is always
present to the Scots mind and is a check upon
gaiety. If in a thoughtless moment you congratulate a Scots mother upon her child with

some freedom of speech, saying, "What a
bonnie bairn that is," the anxious mother will
instantly reply, "Her face is well enough if
her heart was right, but for ony sake be quiet,
for there's no sayin' what may happen. I
never saw a height without a howe." There
is a phrase common on Scots tongues which
illuminates the background of the Scots mind,
and is not intended to be profane, because it
is felt to be true. Any extravagance of
speech or any permissible satisfaction with
success is called a tempting of providence.
The idea is that if we walk humbly and
quietly the unseen powers will leave us alone,
poor creatures of a day, but if we lift our little
heads and make a noise, the inclination to
strike us down will be irresistible.

No man comes off so well at a wedding as
an Englishman, but none is so ill at ease at a
funeral, while a Scotsman has no freedom at
a marriage, since he does not know how the
matter may end, but he carries himself as to
the manner born, with an admirable dignity
and gravity, at a funeral. If it be not a paradox to say it, he delights in funerals and counts
them one of the luxuries of life, for our
piquant sensations may be got from sorrow as

readily as from joy. Upon the ceremonies and the regulations of funerals he is an authority, and is both very learned and very sensitive.

" Peter," says one mourner to his neighbour at the tail of a walking funeral, " div ye see Jamie Thompson walking in the front, side by side wi' the chief mourner, and him no a drop o' blood to the corpse? "

" Fine I see him, a forward, upsettin', ambeetious body; he would be inside the hearse if he could,"— the most awful and therefore most enviable position for a sober-minded Scot.

According, therefore, to the Scots idea, it is more profitable to go to a funeral than to a wedding, and anything that would detract from the chastened satisfaction of such an occasion is deeply resented. And the following conversation between a dying wife and her husband would only be possible in Scotland:

" I've been a guid wife to you, John, a' thae years."

" I'm no denyin', Jean, ye hev'na been a waster. I'll admit ye hae been economical, and verra attentive to the calves and hens."

" Ye'll no refuse me, then, my last request? "

" I will'na, Jean, if it's reasonable, but will hear it first."

" Well, my mither has taken a terrible notion o' gaein' to the funeral, and I canna get her off it.   Noo, John, will ye promise to hev her wi' ye in the first coach? "

" Oh! wooman, ask somethin' else.   I canna do that."

" But, John, I'll never ask onything else o' ye.   Ye micht pit up wi' her, juist for my sake."

" Weel, Jean, if you put it that way, I suppose I maun agree; but I tell you plainly, ye've spoiled the pleasure of the day for me."

It is recorded in an ancient history that there was once a heresy trial, when men were going to be sentenced unto death for denying the orthodox doctrine of the Mass — well-living men, but, no doubt, heretics.   Before sentence was passed one of the prisoners, who had been wearied with many questions, thought that he might in turn ask one of the judges a question.   " My Lord Bishop," he said, " how many wives have you? "   As his Lordship should not have had one even, it was a very searching question, and his Lordship was not prepared with an answer, nor were the other judges anxious to be questioned on their domestic affairs.

There went up from the crowd, it is told, a " sair lauch," as they thought of the bitter mockery of the situation, that such judges should be condemning harmless men, freeborn Scots also, mark you, to death for differing on a mystery no one could understand; at the moral and logical contradiction of it all the spectators sent up their laugh to Heaven. Not the genial, happy laugh of an English crowd tickled by a bit of simple fun from judge or bar, but the fierce raillery of men insulted in reason and outraged in conscience. The men who laughed were not to be trifled with, and their Lordships judged it best to let the prisoners go, that day at least, for when the Scots mob, the most resolute and dangerous to be found anywhere, begins to laugh, it is time for tyrants to hide themselves behind iron doors and the swords of armed men, and even then neither they nor their strongholds might be safe, for this laugh is stronger than steel.

There is therefore no humour so dry and

stringent, with such a bite upon the palate, as that of Scotland, and if there be any bit of it more grim than this, I should like to hear it. An unhappy Scot was condemned to death, after a careful trial, for the murder of his wife under circumstances of considerable provocation, and the verdict was no doubt a just one. There is something good, however, in every man if you walk around him long enough to find it, and his counsel was so much interested in his client that he visited him in the condemned cell.

"There is no hope, Robertson, of a reprieve," said the advocate frankly, "and you know you don't deserve it; but if there is anything else I can do for you, just tell me."

"Well," said Robertson, "I count it very friendly to give me a cry like this, and if ye could get me one thing, I would feel easier on the occasion"— which was a rather felicitous name for the coming function. "Could ye get me ma Sabbath blacks? for I would like to wear them."

"Well," said the advocate, "I daresay I could. But what in the world, Robertson, do you want to wear your Sabbath clothes for on the . . . occasion?"

" I thought maybe you would see that for yourself, sir.   Just as a mark of respect for the deceased."

But I should not wish to part with Scots humour in such a sombre atmosphere as that of my last illustration, and the following is lighter, though still touched beneath the surface with the sense of the awfulness of life.

Among all the ministers of the Scots Kirk perhaps the most characteristic of the last generation was Dr. Norman Macleod, the chaplain of Queen Victoria and the friend of every person in Scotland.   Working-men turned to look at him as he went down the street, saying one to another, " There goes Norman. He's looking well the day."   And when the people strip off a man's title and call him among themselves by his Christian name, then his place is in the people's heart.

One day the minister of the next parish to that of Dr. Macleod was sent for to see a working-man who was dangerously ill. After he had visited him in his bedroom, he came into the kitchen to have some conversation with the man's wife.

" Your husband is very low.   I hope he

may be spared. I am afraid it's typhus fever."

" Aye, aye," the wife replied, with mournful pride. " It's no ordinary trouble."

" I didn't know your husband's face, and I didn't want to ask him questions. Do you attend St. Luke's Church? "

" Na, na," with a fine flavour of contempt both for St. Luke's and its minister; " we gang to Norman's."

" Well, that's all right; you couldn't go to a better. But why did you send for me? "

" Losh bless ye, sir! div ye think that we wad risk Norman wi' typhus fever? "

Whether humour be grim or gay, there are certain conditions by which it ought to be bound in the judgment of all right-thinking folk. It must not be profane, tearing down with a clown's hand the veil which hides the holiest of all in human life, and turning life's great mystery into a petty comedy. It must not be unclean, bringing the blush to the cheek of modesty, or offending the taste of self-respecting people. It must not be cruel, putting the simple to confusion or wounding those who, through their disabilities, suffer enough already. It must be used to brighten the day and make us forget the tedium of the journey; to give us a better understanding of life and its infinite varieties; gentle to chasten innocent foolishness and sharply to rebuke wilful evil-doing. Humour must also be kept in its own place and not be allowed to rob life of its seriousness or speech of its dignity; and we may all lay to heart the story with which George Eliot concludes her timely essay on " Debasing the Moral Currency ":—

" The Tirynthians, according to an ancient story reported by Athenaeus, becoming conscious that their trick of laughter at everything and nothing was making them unfit for the conduct of serious affairs, appealed to the Delphic oracle for some means of cure. The god prescribed a peculiar form of sacrifice, which would be effective if they could carry it through without laughing. They did their best, but the flimsy joke of a boy upset their unaccustomed gravity, and in this way the oracle taught them that even the gods could not prescribe a quick cure for a long vitiation, or give power and dignity to a people who, in a crisis of the public well-being, were at the mercy of a poor jest."

ROBERT BURNS: THE VOICE OF
THE SCOTS PEOPLE

ROBERT BURNS: THE VOICE OF THE SCOTS PEOPLE

WHEN one writes on Robert Burns with the hope of interesting Scots people, one is embarrassed by this double difficulty that the subject of this article presents so many different points of interest, and the audience to whom it is addressed is essentially though justly critical. Both difficulties point to the same solution, and assist a writer in bringing his subject to a focus. I do not, therefore, propose to discuss the technique of Burns's poetry, as, for instance, his metres, or to go into the history of his poems, as, for instance, tracing some of them in their ballad form, or to assign him his place in general literature, or to review the work which he did in English verse and prose. I shall confine myself to one point, and shall speak of Burns as the outcome of the Scots spirit, as the representative of Scots character, as the Lyric Poet of Scots life, as being as nearly as possible the voice of the Scots people. Scotland both in her strength and in her tenderness, Scotland with her virile virtues and her virile faults, not the handful of people at the top of society, not the refuse at the base, not the saints of Scotland, not her rascals either, but the nation, as the nation is, and the nation has done, and the nation has felt, and the nation has suffered, that Scotland speaks out in Burns. He was with emphasis a Scotsman, and stands more perfectly for Scotland than any other writer of the first order. When he wanders into English verse or into English letter writing, he is not himself. " These English songs gravel me to death. I have not the command of the language that I have of my native tongue, in fact I think that my ideas are more barren in English than in Scotch. I have been at ' Duncan Gray ' to dress it in English, but all I can do is desperately stupid." Some of his literary friends at one time advised him to compose in English lest he should cut himself off from the larger public, but both Mr. William Wallace, for whose admirable impartial life of Burns every Scotsman and every reading man should be most thankful, and Matthew Arnold, for whose estimate of

Burns Scotsmen at least are not quite so grateful, both agree that in the English poems we have not the real Burns. The real Burns is the Burns who speaks the Scots dialect.

For the first feature in Burns which one faces is the hardness of his life from beginning to end. " Scarcely ever," says M. Taine, " was seen together more of misery and of talent. He was born January 1759, amid the hoar-frost of a Scottish winter, in a cottage of clay built by his father, a poor farmer of Ayrshire — a sad condition, a sad country, a sad lot. It is hard to be born in Scotland, it is so cold there," concludes the Frenchman. Well, it has been bracing cold and has made strong men, but one may sadly admit it was a cold country for Burns; from his birth to his death he might be said to have lived and died in hoar-frost. One inevitably places Burns side by side with Scott, because the two completely represent Scotland upon all her sides and through all her traditions. Scott is possibly the finest character Scotland has ever produced, a gentleman without reproach and full of charity, and to him Tennyson paid a just tribute —

" Oh! great and gallant Scott,
    True gentleman, heart, blood, and bone,
I would it had been my lot
    To have seen thee and heard thee and known."

Before Scott died he suffered cruelly and
through suffering came to his height; but
Scott belonged to the class which is largely
shielded from hardship: he was not born into
the lot of the common people, and did not
taste of their cup. That cup Burns drank to
its dregs. The difference between English
and Scots character may be referred among
other causes to the bitter struggle which the
Scots race have had with their soil and with
their climate. Mr. Benjamin Swift says,
" The Scotsman expects the worst, even from
God . . .," while " the Englishman sees
no reason for doubting that the Union Jack
is flying at the gates of heaven." Whatever
was arduous in life or in religion Burns ex-
perienced, as he toiled six days of the week
and heard " black Jock Russel " thundering
eternal woe on the seventh. He was brought
up in a home where the wolf was ever at the
door; he served as a ploughman in his early
years; he was unsuccessful as a farmer; he
had finally a poorly paid post in the Excise;

he never knew the meaning of ease; at one time it seemed likely that he would have to emigrate; he had frequently to borrow from his friends; he was afraid lest his body should be seized for debt, and after his death a subscription was raised for his wife and children. He suffered at the hands of his father, whose nature was soured by adversity; and he was insulted by his future father-in-law, who did not judge him worthy of his daughter. He was disappointed of posts he wished to obtain, and he was badly treated by people who ought to have been kind to him. There was hardly any care or humiliation of common life which he did not share, and his life was one long toil from beginning to end, redeemed only by the affection of his wife and the loyalty of a few friends. When Scott visited Ireland in his old age a woman begged alms of him, and when he did not immediately respond she made this plea, " I'm an ould struggler," whereupon Scott turned. " An ould struggler," he said, " and so am I."

Burns did not live to be old; he was worn out soon as many poets have been, but throughout his seven-and-thirty years he was a struggler. He had just one pure satisfaction and that was his work, the inspiration of his soul, and he has described his own battle and his own victory.

> " Now Robin lies in his last lair,
>   He'll gabble rhyme, nor sing nae mair,
>   Cauld poverty, wi' hungry stare,
>   Nae mair shall fear him:
>   Nor anxious fear, nor cankert care,
>   E'er mair come near him.
>
> To tell the truth, they seldom fash't him,
>   Except the moment that they crush't him;
>   For sune as chance or fate has hush't 'em,
>   Tho' e'er sae short,
>   Then wi' a rhyme or sang he lash't 'em,
>   And thought it sport.
>
> Tho' he was bred to kintra wark,
>   And counted was baith wight and stark,
>   Yet that was never Robin's mark
>   To mak a man;
>   But tell him he was learn'd and clark,
>   Ye roos'd him than! "

Akin to the severity of Burns's circumstances was the virility of his character. It has not been for nothing that the thistle was assigned to Scotland as her national emblem and the rose to England, for through all their

history the Scots people have been proud of
their independence, jealous of every neighbour, rooted in their own ways, and difficult
to coerce either in politics or religion. If
they fought within their Kirk — and the Cal-
vinists and Arminians certainly fought hard in
Burns's day — they fought also for their Kirk
and their Kirk for them. If they had some
internal feuds in Scotland, they joined together almost as one man against their " auld
enemie," England. The Scots have been a
democratic people, and Burns is the poet of
democracy. There are two perfect war pieces
in existence, and in both the note is resistance
to tyranny and the victory of liberty. They
are not the jingoism of militarism, or the rant
of the pot-house, they are the song of patriot-
ism; one is " The Marseillaise," which celebrated the deliverance of France from cruel
and foul oppression under which neither the
honour of a woman if she were poor nor the
life of a man if he were a peasant was safe at
the hands of the nobles, and the other is that
war piece which Burns composed in a thun-
derstorm, and which stirs the blood like the
sound of pealing trumpets, " Scots, wha hae
wi' Wallace bled." Burns was not an an-

archist desiring to destroy the foundations of society, else he had not represented an orderly and law-abiding people, neither was he a cringing sycophant trembling before men of high estate. He believed that every man had a right to live and to think for himself, and that the standard of judgment must be not gold and silver, not titles and privileges, but mind and character, or as Burns calls them, sense and worth, and the very heart of the strong Scots folk beats in these verses —

> " A prince can mak a belted knight,
>   A marquis, duke, and a' that;
> But an honest man's aboon his might,
>   Gude faith, he mauna fa' that!
> For a' that, an' a' that,
>   Their dignities an' a' that;
> The pith o' sense, an' pride o' worth,
>   Are higher rank than a' that.

> Then let us pray, that come it may,
>   (As come it will for a' that,)
> That Sense and Worth, o'er a' the earth,
>   Shall bear the gree, an' a' that.
> For a' that, an' a' that,
>   It's comin' yet, for a' that,
> That Man to Man, the world o'er,
>   Shall brothers be for a' that."

Tyranny for Burns was embodied and local-ised in the factor, who has possibly been more detested in Scots country life than either Laird or Lord or any other ruler. Burns never for-got the threatening and insolent epistles which his father used to receive from what he calls the Scoundrel Tyrant, and which Burns de-clares used to reduce the family to tears. He was living then by himself in " the cheerless gloom of a hermit with the unceasing toil of a galley slave," and the " curse was clenched " by the hard hand of the factor. One under-stands what gave the spirit to " Scots wha hae " and " A man's a man for a' that." Burns is thinking of the humiliation and helplessness of a small farmer's home when the hand of the factor descends, and I do not know that the bitterness of the Scots heart when the coun-tryman is trembling for his home before the local tyrant has ever been better described than in one verse of " The Twa Dogs "—

> " I've notic'd, on our laird's court-day,—
> An' mony a time my heart's been wae,—
> Poor tenant bodies, scant o' cash,
> How they maun thole a factor's snash;
> He'll stamp an' threaten, curse an' swear
> He'll apprehend them, poind their gear;

While they maun stan', wi' aspect humble,
An' hear it a', an' fear an' tremble!"

One cannot read the story of the elder Burns's
life, or Burns's own just protest against rural
tyranny, without praying that the day may
soon come when it will not be in the power
of any man to close fifty homes at his will on
a country side and drive forth fifty families of
healthy, contented, loyal, God-fearing people,
that the land be turned into a place of sport,
and let for the amusement of some rich alien.
There will never be perfect freedom in the
land till the people be rooted on the soil, and
the glens and straths of the land which God
has given unto the nation for a heritage be
studded with homes filled with country folk,

"wonderfu' contented,
An' buirdly chiels, an' clever hizzies."

The Jacobitism of Burns, which appears in
some of his most agreeable poems, such as
"Wha hae we gotten for a king, but a wee
bit German lairdie," and "It was a' for our
rightfu' king," is due partly to his heredity,
since his people seem to have been out in the
Fifteen, but partly of variant on the stern

and ineradicable independence of the Scots
people. The Scots are logical in their theology and, although this may seem a paradox,
logical in their politics, for they fought the
Stuarts when they were in power, and then
they fought for them when they were in exile.
They could not abide either home tyranny or
alien tyranny, and being a romantic people
also, the most romantic royal house in history
appealed to their imagination much more than
the Hanoverian Georges. And Burns therefore felt no inconsistency in singing the praises
of the Stuarts in one poem and celebrating the
spirit of the French Revolution in the next.

Burns is distinguished even among poets
by the breadth and depth of his sympathy,
which indeed has no limits and no reserves.
It has not been given to many to have a range
which includes the " Cotter's Saturday
Night," wherein Burns celebrates the excellence of simple family life —

> " To make a happy fireside clime
> To weans and wife,
> That's the true pathos and sublime
> Of human life " —

and " The Jolly Beggars," wherein he sings

with utter abandonment the joys of Bohemian life. Whatever is human appeals to Burns as it did to Shakespeare, and therefore he numbers his clients among all classes, Puritans and Cavaliers, strict livers and free livers together. In the simple annals of the poor there never has been painted a kindlier or purer interior than that poem whose model is " The Farmer's Ingle," by Fergusson, where the priest of the family offers the evening prayer to God —

" The cheerfu' supper done, wi' serious face,
    They, round the ingle, form a circle wide;
The sire turns o'er, with patriarchal grace,
    The big ha'-bible, ance his father's pride;
    His bonnet rev'rently is laid aside,
His lyart haffets wearing thin and bare:
    Those strains that once did sweet in Zion glide,
He wales a portion with judicious care;
And ' Let us worship God!' he says with solemn air."

And truly this is the highest side of Scots life —

" From scenes like these, old Scotia's grandeur springs,
    That makes her lov'd at home, rever'd abroad:
Princes and lords are but the breath of kings,
    ' An honest man's the noblest work of God.' "

It was a genuine and sincere Burns who wrote

those words, and in writing them he celebrated one of the high virtues of his people. It was also the same Burns expressing himself who described that other interior in Poosie-Nansie's lodging-house, where the vagabonds, male and female, are gathered at their supper. In this poem Burns lets himself go, and there is no question he goes at a rattling pace. Many have considered "The Jolly Beggars" the strongest thing which Burns ever did, and it were difficult to mention a piece with such an irresistible swing and so much unreserved sympathy with unredeemed humanity. Upon this piece Matthew Arnold's balanced criticism may be accepted. In "The Jolly Beggars" there is more than hideousness and squalor, there is bestiality; yet the piece is a superb poetic success. It has a breadth, truth, and power which make the famous scene in "Auerbach's Cellar" of Goethe's *Faust* seem artificial and tame beside it, and which are only matched by Shakespeare and Aristophanes —

> " A fig for those by law protected!
> Liberty's a glorious feast!
> Courts for cowards were erected,
> Churches built to please the priest.

> Life is all a variorum,
>   We regard not how it goes;
> Let them cant about decorum,
>   Who have characters to lose."

This one also knows is a side of life, even in the Scotland of the Covenanters.

With nature in her every phase Burns's soul kept tune. With the daisy turned over by the plough on an April day,

> " Wee, modest, crimson-tippèd flow'r,"

in whose doom he sees the fate of an artless maid by love's simplicity betrayed, and the fate of a simple bard,

> " On life's rough ocean luckless starr'd ! "

He feels for the field-mouse, whose little nest had been turned up by the plough,

> " Wee, sleekit, cow'rin, tim'rous beastie " ;

and again he moralises in words better known than the perfect little poem itself —

> " But, Mousie, thou art no thy lane,
>   In proving foresight may be vain ;

> The best-laid schemes o' mice and men
>> Gang aft agley,
> An' lea'e us nought but grief an' pain,
>> For promis'd joy! "

And he is furious as a wounded hare limps by which a fellow had shot —

> " Go live, poor wand'rer of the wood and field,
>> The bitter little that of life remains."

He will write good-humouredly of a creature which is not named in polite society, but which he detected airing itself upon a young lady's bonnet in the kirk, and he points the moral which is often quoted by people who do not know the subject of the poem —

> " O wad some power the giftie gie us
>> To see oursels as ithers see us!
> It wad frae mony a blunder free us,
>> An' foolish notion:
> What airs in dress an' gait wad lea'e us,
>> An' ev'n devotion! "

He has a kindly thought for saints and sinners, for beasts and men, for vermin and for outcasts, for witches, and even the enemy of us all is not outside his charity.   And I will not say that Burns has not stirred an unconfessed echo in certain hearts with a last verse of his " Address to the Deil "—

> " But fare-you-weel, auld ' Nickie-ben '!
> O wad ye tak a thought an' men'!
> Ye aiblins might — I dinna ken —
>   Still hae a stake:
> I'm wae to think upo' yon den,
>   Ev'n for your sake!"

His sympathy with the wounded and the helpless was quite consistent with his merciless satire of unreality and hypocrisy, and therein he was a true Scot, for irony is the characteristic form of Scots humour. One can taste it in the poets before the Reformation, like Sir David Lindsay of the Mount, in Knox's History of the Reformation, and in modern days in Thomas Carlyle. The flavour is not wanting in Stevenson and Barrie, but there is only a faint suggestion in Scott, as for instance in that pious smuggling merchant of *Redgauntlet*. It is a pronounced and appetising trait in Scots literature, and survives pleasantly in a distinguished Edinburgh newspaper, which every Scotsman away from home reads with the greater relish because it has in

its columns a breath of the snell east wind.
Whether it be Lindsay or Burns, the subject
of satire in Scots letters is almost always the
Kirk, and this is not because the Scots are ir-
religious, or because the Kirk has been alien,
but very largely because the Kirk has played
such a part in the history of Scotland. The
nation and the Kirk have been one, and the
history of the people has been largely shaped
by the Kirk; she has been a guardian of Scots
liberty in many a crisis, but she has also been
a very severe nurse of her children. The
Kirk and Burns had their own special quarrel
in which no one can justify the conduct of
Burns, and it may be admitted that the Kirk
was not very wise in her treatment of him.
Apart, however, from any provocation which
he gave to the guardian of morals in the land,
the Kirk in the eighteenth century, or perhaps
one may say conventional religion, presented
two vulnerable points which a satirist could
not resist attacking. Hypocrisy in its ele-
mentary sense of the double life had been
raised to the level of genius, when a man like
Lord Grange spent days in affecting exercises
of penitence before the sacrament, and other
days in immoral orgies. An extreme Calvin-

ism was also preached which was an offence both to the reason and to the conscience, and one can easily trace the connection between the high doctrine and the low morals, since many were convinced that, as they were the elect of God's purpose, they could do as they pleased with His commandments. This was the national scandal which Burns pilloried in his "Address to the Unco Guid," and his description of the "Holy Fair," which was said to have been drawn to the life, and in the most biting piece that came from his pen, where indeed the parchment was the flesh of a man, "Holy Willie's Prayer." Rabbi Duncan used to say that there was only one heresy, and that was Antinomianism, which really means that if a man holds the right creed he may live any kind of life, and this destructive delusion was never scarified in literature with such final success as in the prayer offered by the sanctimonious and evil living Ayrshire elder.

Antinomianism is pierced through the heart as with a dart when this worthless wretch lifts up his voice in all confidence —

> "O Thou, who in the heavens does dwell,
>   Who, as it pleases best Thysel',
>   Sends ane to heaven an' ten to hell,

A' for Thy glory,
And no for ony guid or ill
They've done afore Thee!

I bless and praise Thy matchless might,
When thousands Thou hast left in night,
That I am here afore Thy sight,
For gifts an' grace
A burning and a shining light
To a' this place."

With this severity there has always gone in Scots character an underlying tenderness, and one makes bold to say that Strong as Burns was in that fierce satire which played like a flame of fire round the moral faults of his people, he came to his height not in bitterness but in kindness, not in comedy but in pathos. Matthew Arnold, with all his fine insight, made several memorable mistakes in criticism, and I think he was not perfectly just in his treatment of Burns. He gives him a high place, allowing that although his " world of Scotch drink, Scotch religion, and Scotch manners is against a poet," while the world of Chaucer is fairer, richer, more significant than that of the Ayrshire poet, yet Burns " is by far the greater force." He insists, however, that Burns is

wanting in that note of high seriousness which
is the infallible mark of the great classics.
Arnold admits that Burns is not deficient in
the sense of the tears of things, and one would
hold that he has established his place among
those who have worthily and poignantly de-
picted the tragedy of life in " Ae Fond Kiss,
and then we sever," for has the vain regret
ever been so perfectly expressed as in these
lines —

> " Had we never lov'd sae kindly,
> Had we never lov'd sae blindly,
> Never met, or never parted,
> We had ne'er been broken-hearted "—

or in " Auld Lang Syne," especially in the
two verses —

> " We twa hae run about the braes,
> And pu'd the gowans fine;
> But we've wander'd mony a weary foot
> Sin auld lang syne.
>
> We twa hae paidl'd i' the burn,
> From mornin' sun till dine;
> But seas between us braid hae roar'd
> Sin auld lang syne."

It seems to me that in another poem which it is
true Burns did not so much create as adapt,

and which is much less widely known, Burns comes quite as near to the heart of things as any man who ever wrote, and I think it is worth full quotation —

"It was a' for our rightfu' King
    We left fair Scotland's strand;
It was a' for our rightfu' King
    We e'er saw Irish land,
            My dear;
    We e'er saw Irish land.

Now a' is done that men can do,
    And a' is done in vain;
My love and native land fareweel,
    For I maun cross the main,
            My dear;
    For I maun cross the main.

He turn'd him right and round about
    Upon the Irish shore;
And gae his bridle-reins a shake,
    With adieu for evermore,
            My dear;
    With adieu for evermore.

The soger frae the wars returns,
    The sailor frae the main;
But I hae parted frae my love,
    Never to meet again,
            My dear;
    Never to meet again.

When day is gane, and night is come,
    And a' folk bound to sleep;
I think on him that's far awa',
    The lee-lang night and weep,
        My dear;
    The lee-lang night and weep."

Matthew Arnold, in spite of certain disabilities for the criticism of Burns, has done him
on the whole so much justice that it may seem
ungrateful to complain, but one must insist
that if sincerity be the criterion of classical
poetry, Burns is not wanting.

Here one is tempted to turn aside from the
main road and make a brief comparison between Burns and that English poet who essayed the same task, and who owed himself so
much to Burns. Wordsworth set himself to
sing, "Of joy in widest commonalty spread,"
and he certainly has dealt with common life
simply. There are those who object to poetry
being mixed up with philosophy and on that
account disparage Wordsworth, and there are
those who profess themselves unable to distinguish his poetry from prose, and who per-
mit themselves to make play with Wordsworth. On the other hand, a select number of
fine minds, fine perhaps rather than strong,

have always taken Wordsworth for a prophet, and one critic firmly believes that the poetical performance of Wordsworth is, " after that of Shakespeare, the most considerable in our language from the Elizabethan age to the present time."

Both Burns and Wordsworth dealt with country life, both wrote plainly, both pointed their moral, both had their message, and one need not ask which is the greater — it is enough for us to note the difference of temperament. Wordsworth's gentle meditative verse is like a garden lake with goldfish swimming in it, Burns's strong stirring lines like the mountain torrent carrying everything before it. Wordsworth is a pleasure ground with simple flowers laid out in beds, but Burns is the mountain side with the billows of purple heather. One cannot forget that when Burns met Scott, who was only then a lad, the poet discerned coming greatness in him, and laying his hand upon his head conveyed to him the grace of literary succession. When Wordsworth visited Scott he received with much complacency Scott's generous tributes, but had not the heart to make any return. And when Scott went out upon one of his rambles, Wordsworth remained in the house in order to listen to the reading of his own poems.   Each poet has had his own reward; Wordsworth's mission has been to an esoteric circle of self-conscious cultured people and anæmic ecclesiastics, while Burns has been the poet of the people, and with his verse so arch, so winsome, so tender, so merry, has thrust a song into the mouth of the man who holds the plough and the woman who milks the cow. No nation has such love-songs as Burns has given Scotland in " My luve's like a red, red rose," " The rigs o' barley," " Green grow the rashes, O! "   " O whistle and I'll come to ye, my lad," " Comin' thro' the rye," besides many more, or such songs of pathos as " To Mary in Heaven," " Ye banks and braes o' bonnie Doon," " John Anderson, my Jo," and " Auld Lang Syne."   It is his glory and his claim upon national gratitude that he has made a proud and reserved people articulate, and has taught them to sing their loves and their wars in lines which have few rivals in the lyric poetry of the world.

When one is celebrating Burns, and espe-cially when touching on his love-songs, one remembers Lord Rosebery's words concerning

" the eternal controversy which no didactic oil will ever assuage, as to Burns's private life and morality." There are those who have done their best to minimise his faults, and I sympathise with the pious effort of Mr. William Wallace in that direction, and there are those who dwell upon his faults with gusto, and that is why one resents certain passages in the appreciation of Burns which concludes the very scholarly edition of Henley and Henderson. Why should Burns be specially selected for the pillory while the sins of other famous men are passed over?

This is a question which Lord Rosebery very justly asks, but which he does not answer. Probably the causes for this unwelcome discussion are, the close connection between Burns's poetry and his life, his poetry portraying its most deplorable passages in autobiography; and the other reason is that the Scots Kirk was in the eighteenth century a severe censor of morals, and Burns was not able to sin in private. There never were such Pharisees as in that century, and therefore there never was a more bold Bohemian than Burns. One does not wish to linger on the subject, but I would offer with diffidence two remarks, certainly not by way of apology for evil living, but in order to place Burns's character in its right light. We cannot apply the same standard of judgment to every man, we must make some allowance for temperament, and especially for the rich and hot blood of poets from David to Burns. It would have been better without doubt for the world, for Jerusalem long ago, and for Ayrshire in the eighteenth century, if those two poets had been men of cold nature and prim respectability. They would not have sinned and they would not have suffered, and it is likely that they would not have written their masterpieces. Concerning their sinning one is inclined to quote the saying of a great Church Father regarding the fall of man, " O beata culpa." The passion which sent Burns into the far country opened his mouth in song, which is one of the arresting paradoxes of human nature.

One also would like to remind the public that Burns was not a sheer Bohemian, and to protest against the idea that unredeemed profligacy is a necessary condition of literary work. He was not a Scots Verlaine whose life was one course of foul living, abject pauperism, and occasional crime, varied by fits of remorse and a fine play of genius. Burns worked hard both in youth and manhood, he celebrated in undying verse the foolishness of sin and the virtues of domestic life. Amid a conflict of temptation he married Jean Armour, and was on the whole a kind husband to her, and a good father to his children. The faults of his early youth were many, and he never was a model of flawless perfection, but he was true to the great tradition of Scotland in magnifying the home, and his own home he dearly loved.

When one tries to estimate Burns's place, not in general literature, which is beyond the scope of this article, but in the Scots department, he has to guard against two ensnaring tendencies. One is so to emphasise his originality as to leave him a solitary phenomenon — an Ayrshire ploughman who by miraculous inspiration suddenly opened his mouth and burst into undying song, a Melchizedec in literature without father or mother, beginning or end of days. The other is to treat him as simply a ballad improver taking old Scots verses and setting them in order. In fact there is no man without an ancestry and few

are without descendants.   No great poet has
ever been the echo of other people, and yet
no great poet could detach himself from the
past.   Burns was, in the genuine sense of the
Scots   word   for   poet,   "a   maker."   He
brought a mind of singular freshness and a
genius of marked individuality to his work.
It is also true that there stretched behind him
a line of Scots poets, writing in a dialect
which connects them with Chaucer. Burns
had   his   distant   ancestry   in   Lindsay,
Montgomery, and Dunbar, and his nearer
forebears in Sempill, Allan Ramsay, and poor
unfortunate Robert Fergusson, whose grave
Burns watered with tears, and whose tomb he
built.   Many of Burns's finest poems are
based on ballads which passed from mouth to
mouth among the Scots people, just as Shakespeare obtained the plots of his plays from
many quarters, and Chaucer reproduces Boccaccio, while that great Italian was himself
only a collector.   As Burns has been justly
censured for the coarseness of certain verses,
let it be never forgotten that every ancient
ballad which he touched he purified, so that
much Scots song which otherwise would have
to-day been buried out of sight, having passed

through Burns's hands like tainted water through a gravel bed, has flowed in purity into the main stream of literature. When Burns began to write, Scots literature was dead, for the brilliant Edinburgh school, Hume the philosopher, and Robertson the historian, and Blair the critic, were not writers of Scots literature, but Scotsmen in English literature. Burns was the heir of the national tradition, and he also was its climax. Perhaps there one must correct himself: he relit the torch of vernacular speech, and he passed it on to Scott, ordained by Burns as his successor.

One may never forget Burns's visit to Edinburgh, which is always a superior city, but was then to the last degree high and mighty. I do not say that Edinburgh treated Burns badly, for it showed him much kindness, and I do not say that Burns did not impress Edinburgh, for people never forgot his eyes, which glowed like coals of fire, and men like Dugald Stewart were enthusiastic about his conversation. But one is immensely tickled by the attitude of the Edinburgh critics to the Ayrshire poet, which was one of good-natured patronage. Dr. Hugh Blair, whose chief effort

in criticism was affirming the authenticity of
Macpherson's Ossian, and who was a figure of
self-satisfied gentility, wrote a letter to Burns,
which is altogether delightful, on the poet's
return to Ayrshire. "You are now, I pre-
sume," says the old gentleman, " to retire to a
more private walk of life, and I trust will conduct yourself there with industry, prudence,
and honour. In the midst of those employ-
ments which your situation will render proper,
you will not, I hope, neglect to promote public esteem by cultivating your genius." And
so on, concerning which one can only remark,
that the idea of Dr. Blair patting Burns on the
back is prodigious.

One is much interested in hearing Burns
upon Blair. " In my opinion," says the poet,
" Dr. Blair is merely an astonishing proof of
what industry and application can do; he has
a heart not of the finest water, but far from being an ordinary one; in short, he is a truly
worthy and most respectable character." Admirable! That was just Dr. Blair —" a most
respectable character "; and when it is remembered that Blair, besides many lucrative posts,
such as minister of the High Kirk and Pro-
fessor of Rhetoric in the University of Edin-

burgh, enjoyed a pension of £200 per year for
his literary attainments, one wishes that Robert
Burns had been as kindly treated.   Poetry is
not reckoned a remunerative form of literature, and true poets are themselves rare.   Why
should any poet like Burns be left to toil and
starve?   One would not like to think of Burns
as a poet laureate, a kind of higher servant attached to a palace, who comes at the summons
of a bell, and takes directions about an ode on a
birth or a marriage, but one would have been
thankful if Pitt, who, as Lord Rosebery points
out, passed on Burns " one of his rare and
competent literary judgments," had placed the
Scots poet beyond the reach of want, and since
it was his lot to die young, had at least secured
that Burns should have peace in his last days.
But there is a just fate, and Blair had his
good things in his own day and is now unread.
Burns tasted little else but misery and now
has come into his kingdom.   " Don't be
afraid," Burns said to his wife, " I'll be more
respected a hundred years after I am dead
than I am at present."   The hundred years
have more than passed, and Burns's hope has
been more than fulfilled.   While he lived
Scotland had begun to love her chief poet,

and now there is none born of woman, in her long history, whom Scotland loves more dearly, for Robert Burns was bone of her bone and flesh of her flesh. He shared the lot of the people to its last grain in his labours, his sufferings, his sorrows, his sins. He has told what the people think and feel, and love and hate. An imperfect man, a sinning and foolish man if you please, but one of the twelve great poets of the human race, and in every drop of his blood, and in every turn of his thought, the poet of Scotland. We remember the joy he has brought to our lives, and the expression he has given to our sorrow. We remember how he stirs us as no other voice in poetry. And for the rest of it, to quote a passage of wise charity from a delightful book of letters published within recent years, " the most wholesome attitude is to be grateful for what in the way of work, of precept, of example these men achieved, and to leave the mystery of their faults to their Maker in the noble spirit of Gray's ' Elegy '—

> ' No farther seek his merits to disclose,
>   Or draw his frailties from their dread abode
> (There they alike in trembling hope repose),
>   The bosom of his Father and his God.' "

Burns himself was ever anticipating his trial at the bar of human judgment, and he made his own irresistible plea for frail mortal man in the immortal words —

> " Then gently scan your brother Man,
>   Still gentler sister Woman;
> Tho' they may gang a kennin wrang,
>   To step aside is human:
> One point must still be greatly dark,
>   The moving WHY they do it;
> And just as lamely can ye mark,
>   How far perhaps they rue it."

WAVERLEY NOVELS

WAVERLEY NOVELS

ENGLISH literature, with all its wealth of genius, does not afford another body of fiction so wide in its historical range, so varied in its types of character, so genial in its humanity as the series of romances which will be known while our speech lasts by the felicitous title of the *Waverley Novels* — felicitous not merely because it is a good-sounding word, but because in *Waverley* Scott struck the characteristic note of his fiction. From *Waverley,* which appeared on the 7th July 1814, with an impression of one thousand copies, to *Castle Dangerous,* which was published at the close of November 1831, with an introduction sent from Naples in February 1832, was a period of seventeen years and twenty-seven books. Some of them were written at white heat, the last two volumes of *Waverley* in three weeks; some of them were written in agonising pain, as, for instance, *The Bride of Lammermoor;* many were written to pay a debt of honour. After the *Fair Maid of Perth* the first French critic of our day considers a rapid decline and symptoms of exhaustion were observed, and the same writer believes that in dying Sir Walter had not taken with him any great unfinished idea. " He had said enough for his glory and our delight . . . for the whole civilised world, a generous wizard and a kindly bene- factor." From *Count Robert of Paris,* which is cast in the decadence of the Byzan- tine period —" the tame worn-out civilisation of those European Chinese "— and was a burden which poor Scott's now " staggering penmanship " could not carry, to *St. Ronan's Well,* which was contemporary with himself, embraces seven centuries. To the age of chivalry belong *The Betrothed, The Talis- man,* and *Ivanhoe.* The fourteenth century has the *Fair Maid of Perth,* and the fifteenth is represented by *Quentin Durward.* To the sixteenth century are assigned *The Abbot* and *The Monastery* and *Kenilworth,* while the seventeenth lives before us in *Woodstock* and *Peveril of the Peak* for England and *Old Mortality* and the *Legend of Montrose* for Scotland. The eighteenth century is richly endowed by *The Pirate,* the *Heart of Midlo-*

thian, Waverley, and *Redgauntlet* and *Rob Roy.* It is an achievement of the first order to travel through so many ages and in so many lands with unfailing sympathy and the most intimate touch, so that whatever be the value of Scott's history in the eyes of modern criticism, nothing human was strange to him and everything human was made to live in his pages. As Frederic Harrison, one of the most eloquent of our English critics, has said: " We see the dawn of our English nation, the defence of Christendom against the Koran, the grace and terror of Feudalism, the rise of monarchy out of baronies, the rise of Parliaments of monarchy, the rise of industry out of serfage, the pathetic ruin of chivalry, the splendid death struggle of Catholicism, the sylvan tribes of the mountains (remnants of our prehistoric forefathers) beating themselves to pieces against the hard advance of modern industry. We see the grim heroism of the Bible martyrs, the catastrophe of feudalism overwhelmed by a practical age which knew little of its graces and almost nothing of its virtues."

It was the distinction of Scott more, perhaps, than any other writer, to originate the

" renaissance of wonder " in the nineteenth century, and his novels must be judged, not by the standard of historical science, but from the standpoint of imagination. It is perfectly true that he places Shakespeare's plays in the mouths of men when, as some one pleasantly remarks, Shakespeare was hardly old enough to rob an orchard, and on the other hand he will make Shakespeare die twenty years before his time. When Dr. Dryasdust starts to examine Scott's romances with a microscope, I am prepared to believe he will find a thousand inaccuracies in minute detail and also some intrepid handling of the larger facts, and I would offer this advice to the young student of history, when he is intent on dates and facts, to close his Scott and give diligent ear to Freeman and Creighton and Gardiner, and amongst contemporary Scotsmen to Hume Brown and Hay Fleming and that fine young scholar, Mr. Rait. If you desire to be introduced to the men and women who made history and to see them live and move, not pictures on a wall but actors on a stage, till you catch the glint of the eye and the flush on the face, till you hear the burst

of passion and start at the sudden glow, till
the tears come to your eyes at the real tragedy, and you laugh aloud at the pleasant comedy, then turn to this theatre where the play-
ers are ever at their best because they are simply human, and the play never wearies because it deals with the perennial drama of
humanity. When we desire to pass a measured judgment upon the political or religious
principles of any period, then must we seek
some other teacher than this romanticist, but
we have our own debt to pay to him. At the
wave of his magical wand, knights rise before
us in their steel armour; loyal blundering
Cavaliers drink " a health to King Charles ";
grim fighting Covenanters sing their Psalm
as they face Claverhouse's dragoons; absent-
minded, kind-hearted antiquaries discourse
on their discoveries; hard-handed Scots,
soldiers of fortune like Dugald Dalgetty and
Balafré, and broken, thieving caterans like
Rob Roy. No one has ever given such a vivid
likeness of King James VI., our Scots Solo-
mon, with his awkward body, his foolish
mouth, his undoubted learning, his timid nature, his kind heart, his mean ways, and his

amazing self-conceit, and every student of
morals must be grateful for his masterly study
of Louis XI., so orthodox, superstitious,
treacherous, cruel, able, a man of rat-like cunning, set amongst the gallant and honourable
gentlemen of his court.

Mr. Maurice Hewlett has delighted us with
an artistic portrait of Queen Mary, but there
is not in the *Queen's Quair* any passage so
commanding as that when Mary in Loch
Leven Castle is reminded by tactless Lady
Fleming of a certain masque in Holyrood;
and while many a modern novelist has tried
his hand upon King Charles II., it is in
Peveril of the Peak we get our most vivacious
picture of the charming manners, imperturb-
able good nature, political astuteness, unrec-
ognised cleverness, and unblushing immorality of the Merry Monarch. It sometimes oc-
curs to one that no writer has ever done more
absolute justice to the Stuarts than Sir Walter, and none has felt more evidently the romantic charm of that ill-fated house. He is
indeed in the first line of the great creative
minds of the world, for he has " definitely
succeeded in the ideal reproduction of historical types so as to preserve at once beauty, life,

and truth," a task which a sound critic declares " not even Shakespeare himself entirely achieved."

Out of this large and wealthy place, the world of men, in which Scott was as much at home as Shakespeare, Scotland was that province where he was most familiar and where his hand was firmest. " There is," said La Rochefoucauld, " a country accent, not in speech only, but in thought, conduct, character, and manner of existing, which never forsakes a man," and no Scotsman was more entirely Scots than Sir Walter. What he did not know about Scotland, with one or two notable exceptions on which I shall touch, is not knowledge. He had gone through the length and breadth of the land, and had met after a friendly fashion with all conditions. Pawky Scots provosts like him of Dumfries, who was a plain-spoken man, and kept right with both sides, advising Allan Fairford to keek into his letter of introduction before he delivered it, and hurrying off to the Council lest Bailie Laurie should be " trying some of his manœuvres "; Bailie Nicol Jarvie, so innocently charged with self-importance, and so fearful that Bailie Graham should get a

hold of the night's proceedings in the prison;
border sheep farmers like big Dandie Dinmont, ready for a fight with a neighbour
either at the fair or in the Law Courts, but
scornful of the idea that he should take away
his neighbour's land; local factors like Macwheeble, keeping together with hard toil
their foolish clients' estates; Highland chiefs
like M'Ivor, poor, proud, and passionate, yet
loyal to their cause and to their kinsmen;
country gossips like Meg Dods, the masterful
hostess of the Cleikum Inn; pragmatical
servants full of argument and advice, like
Richie Moniplies and Andrew Fairservice;
theological peasants, unwearied in controversy and matchless in distinctions, like
David Deans; judges, advocates, sheriffs,
sheriff-substitutes, country writers, school-
masters, ministers, beggars, fisher-folk, gip-
sies, Highland clansmen, country lairds,
great nobles. How distinct, how vivid, how
convincing is each person in his album; as
you turn the pages you identify the likeness
by the representatives you have known yourself. Scott's novels have been translated into
every civilised tongue, and Scott has become
the most valuable commercial asset of his

country, for the ends of the earth come to see the land of which he is the cicerone, and every third American is a lineal descendant of Queen Mary. With the United States as an annex of Scotland, through the conquering genius of Sir Walter, one may not make an exclusive boast, but apart from Americans, he may believe that Scott's genius reached its height in the novels of his own country, and that only a Scot can appreciate the confident and faultless skill with which he etches the character of his people.

Stevenson caught the romantic colour of Scots life, and could describe it with a distinction of style to which our author had no claim, and in his *Weir of Hermiston* Stevenson has given us a powerful Northern type of the morose order, but he was not in touch with ordinary life, as Sir Walter was. With Stevenson the people are apt to be picturesque figures, whom he has lighted on and brought into his study as artists find inspiration by accident, and turn it to account. With Scott they are gossips, men and women whom he has known, on the Tweed and the borders. He does not thrust exquisitely turned phrases into their mouths, but he lets them talk, and is

pleased because they say the things which interest him.   One class only was alien to him,
the mercantile class, which was finding itself
and coming into its kingdom, and passing re-
form bills, and doing a hundred things which
Scott did not appreciate.   He gives a kindly
part to " Jingling Geordie," because Heriot
was a benefactor to his country, and did not
pass from his own place at the beginning of
the seventeenth century.   And he deals pleasantly with the Glasgow Bailie, but one knows
that he sympathises with Rob Roy's contemptuous rejection of a place in the Bailie's
business for one of the young Macgregors.
Scott did not set himself down to write the
novel with a purpose, and his stories owe part
of their charm to the fact that they are not
studies in theology or the sexual question, but
consciously or unconsciously they teach his
gospel about society.   When Carlyle complained that our highest literary man had no
message whatever to deliver to the world he
really is beside the mark, for Scott was
charged in the marrow of his bones, as Carlyle
used to say, with a creed, and it was one
which Carlyle detested.   Every novelist of
the front rank who has produced an organic

body of fiction, whether Balzac or Thackeray, Flaubert or Zola, has a spinal cord running through his books. It may not be carried to the tedious length of Balzac, or the pedantic genealogies of Zola, but it dominates the whole and is the pervading spirit. With Scott it was the ancient and dying spirit of feudalism. He was a stranger to the struggle of the times; he was a lover of past ages. His is the charm of autumn, the delicate colouring of a summer that is over. He touched no question of religious doubt and stood for the simplicity of faith, and one knows he is speaking for himself in the unquestioning reverence of his cavaliers for authority, and the submission of Scots peasants to their ministers. According to his idea, society was a graded order (he ought to have been the novelist of the " Young England " school) wherein each rank found its recognised place, and had its own privileges in subordination to the whole. George IV. was, in this simple faith, an almost supernatural personage, and the humble enthusiastic loyalty with which he welcomed that obese and very vulgar monarch to Scotland would have greatly delighted the cynical humour of

Thackeray and shows how perfectly qualified
Scott was to appreciate a cavalier's attitude
to Charles II.   The Duke of Buccleuch was
his chief, whose sorrows he shared as his own,
and whose recognition, whenever the Duke
was pleased to write to him, he deeply valued.
For himself, he belonged to the gentry, the
third order after the King and the nobility,
and above the farmers and the tradesmen.
With him were lawyers and soldiers and the
professional classes generally.   For some reason he took little notice of medical men, and
indeed has only one good doctor in his Scots
novels (the apothecary in the *Fair Maid of
Perth* is detestable), and although he is altogether admirable, I do not think that Gideon
Grey has touched the popular imagination.
It has been a bad tradition in literature either
to ignore or to depreciate the most beneficent
of professions, and one is thankful for the
slender mercy of *The Surgeon's Daughter*.
Each class in society was to be preserved in
its proper rights so long as it remained in its
own sphere.

Scott was most friendly with his inferiors
and most respectful to his superiors — ever on
the understanding that he knew his place and

they knew theirs. No person in his novels
rises and is made a hero because he has
climbed from poverty to riches. The self-
made man hardly appears, and when he does,
he is treated contemptuously. Christie
Steele, the prejudiced old housekeeper of the
Croftangrys, acknowledged that Mr. Treddle's mill had given employment in the dis-
trict, but Mr. Treddle's efforts to be a country gentleman only excited her acidulous humour. When Mr. Gilbert Glossin, the country lawyer in *Guy Mannering,* conciliates the
pompous baronet and obtains a most conde-
scending invitation to dinner, the achievement
is understood to reflect credit on Glossin's
adroitness. And Sir Arthur Wardour is furious when a lawyer addresses him in a letter as
" Dear Sir "—" He will be calling me ' Dear
Knight' next." The Lord Keeper in *The
Bride of Lammermoor* had scrambled up to
his high position from a low estate, and therefore he is a timid and propitiatory man, ill
at ease among country sports, and afraid in
the presence of the haughty young lord, who
on his part, poverty-stricken but ancient born,
dominates the Lord Keeper, as a hawk would
terrify a barn-door fowl. Lady Ashton, on

the other hand, one detests for her cruelty, but respects for her courage — the difference was that she had good blood in her veins. Dugald Dalgetty was a sturdy old blade and carried a conscience in him, for he would never take service with the other side till his time had expired with their opponents; he was a man of his hands, too, and one of the most vivid scenes in all Scott's work is Dugald seizing the Duke of Argyll in his castle.   But Dalgetty shows badly beside the Highland chiefs, because, although he was a cock laird in Aberdeenshire, you can see that after all he was only a "body."   Although Scott laughs at Lady Margaret Bellenden for her aristocratic prejudices and her recurring allusions to Charles II., he has a sneaking fondness for her, and drew her character from some of the old Jacobite ladies he knew; and although he makes play with Baron Bradwardine, with his family tree, bears, boot-jack and all, yet you feel that he would be just as much concerned about his own pedigree.   He believes in the better class showing kindness to the poorer, and there is an atmosphere everywhere of good cheer, but it is the kindness of a chief to his clansmen.   His men drink, and perhaps put away as much as Dickens's heroes, which is saying a great deal, but they drink like gentlemen, not like grooms.   Mrs. Gamp is very taking, and a philosopher in her own way, but she would be quite out of place in the *Waverley Novels*.   There are homely women in them, and Meg Dods had all Mrs. Gamp's force of character and native resolution, but no person is vulgar.   Among all his peasants I do not remember one, with the doubtful exception of worthy Andrew Fairservice, who is mean.   His poor Highlanders, the "Dougal cratur" and the rest of them, and his Lowland ploughmen, Cuddie Headrigg, for instance, all command respect, as sound-minded and able-bodied men, just as much as their masters in their place.   One of the finest and most discriminating things Scott ever did is the story of the two drovers, where the basal difference between the Highland and the Lowland character is admirably drawn, so that any one who reads it will understand that there is a gulf between, say a Yorkshire man and a Ross-shire man.   They have different virtues and different vices, their blood runs at a different heat, and their eyes look on a different world.   Scott rose to

his height, and his imagination burned with
its purest flame, when he describes the loyalty
of a Highlander to his chief. " I was only
ganging to say, my lord," said Evan Mac-
combich, when both his chief and he had been
condemned to death at Carlisle Assizes, " that
if your excellent honour and the honourable
Court would let Vich Ian Vohr go free just
this once, and let him gae back to France, and
no to trouble King George's government
again, that ony six o' the very best of his clan
will be willing to be justified in his stead; and
if you'll just let me gae down to Glennaquoich
I'll fetch them up to ye mysell, to head or
hang, and you may begin wi' me the very first
man."   And when a sort of laugh was heard
in the Court, Evan looked round sternly.
" If the Saxon gentlemen are laughing," he
said, " because a poor man such as me, thinks
my life or the life of six of my degree, is
worth that of Vich Ian Vohr, it's like enough
they may be very right; but if they laugh because they think I would not keep my word,
and come back to redeem him, I can tell them
they ken neither the heart of a Hielandman,
nor the honour of a gentleman."   He disliked
the change from the old to the new, when the

Treddles supplant the Croftangrys, and also new-fangled fashions, and would rather share the feudal and homely hospitality of Lord Huntingtower's house in the *Fortunes of Nigel,* than go with his profligate son, Lord Dalgarno, to the French eating-house and the gambling table. A clear distinction is drawn between the two apprentices in the same novel, because the one is only a London trader's son, and the other belongs to a poor, but gentle Northern house.

Some one was recently denouncing an ingenuous woman writer, beloved of shop-girls, and declaring her to be immoral, and his ground was that she was fond of marrying the shop-girl to the lord, or some other achievement of the same kind. Scott certainly was cleansed from all immorality of this kind (with the inevitable solitary exception), and no woman of gentle birth marries beneath her in Scott, and no man aspires to a woman above him. They marry and give in marriage each within his own degree. It is true that pretty Peggy Ramsay in the *Fortunes of Nigel* does become Lady Glenvarloch, but this exigency of the story is relieved by establishing some connection between the clockmaker's daughter and the great Dalhousie family. If Morton in *Old Mortality* marries Miss Bellenden, it is to be remembered he is an officer's son, although his father was a mean old laird, and that he does not marry her till he himself is a distinguished officer. The line between gentlefolk and the rest of creation is kindly, quietly, but constantly and firmly drawn.

His feudal gospel affords a more engaging illustration for the majority of people when he treats, as he loves to do, of the loyalty of a servant to his master. One of his most delightful minor creations is the " Dougal cratur," the type of dog-like fidelity. When he thinks it wise to fling up his post as turnkey in Glasgow gaol, he is careful to leave the doors unlocked so that his chief and Bailie Nicol Jarvie may not be caught in a trap, and when the Bailie is sore put to it in the publichouse, Dugald jumped up from the floor with his native sword and target in his hand to do battle for the discomfited magistrate. " Her nainsell has eaten the town pread at the Cross o' Glasgow, and py her troth she'll fight for Bailie Sharvie at the Clachan of Aberfoyle — tat will she e'en! " Macwheeble was

an abject and a worm of the dust, and one of
the drollest scenes in Scott's vein of humour
is the worthy man wishing to take charge of
Vich Ian Vohr's purse on the campaign and to
lay the money out at interest; and there's no
end to the scheming and parsimony of the
Bailie, but there was the honest feudal heart
hid away beneath the dirt and dross. "If I
fall, Macwheeble," said his master, Bradwardine, "you have all my papers and know
all my affairs; be just to Rose," whereat the
worthy factor set up a lamentable howl. "If
that doleful day should come while Duncan
Macwheeble had a boddle it should be Miss
Rose's. He would scroll for a plack or she
kenn'd what it was to want." And Scott has
fewer more cunning scenes than Waverley's
visit to Macwheeble when the war was over,
and Macwheeble was suspiciously watching
every visitor. For a while he listened to
Waverley with anxiety lest he had come to
claim assistance, was greatly cheered when he
heard that it was well with him, and when he
declared his intention of sharing his fortune
with Miss Rose Bradwardine, the Bailie rose
to his height. "He flung his best wig out
of the window because the block on which it

was placed stood in the way of his career,
chucked his cap to the ceiling, caught it as it
fell; whistled Tullochgorum; danced a Highland fling with inimitable grace and agility,
and then threw himself exhausted into a chair
exclaiming, " Lady Wauverley! — ten thousand a year, the least penny! Lord preserve
my poor understanding." And after making
a hurried note on a sheet of paper, " a sma'
minute to prevent parties fra resiling," he
broke forth again. " Lady Wauverley, ten
thousand a year! Lord be gude unto me
. . . it dings Balmawhapple out and out,
a year's rent worth of Balmawhapple, fee and
life rent, Lord make us thankful." Bradwardine himself lies concealed on his own estate and not a tenant will betray him, and he
often finds " bits of things in my way that the
poor bodies, God help them, put there because they think they may be useful to me."
Richie Moniplies is a preaching and provoking fool of a man-servant, but he is unflinch-
ingly loyal to Nigel, and therefore Scott gives
him a knighthood before he has done with
him. Edie Ochiltree, the beggar man, when
there is a threatening of invasion, lends a hand
for the defence of the land he loves, and
proves himself a dog of the old Scots breed —

a fighting terrier — and not the shiftless, treacherous, cowardly tramp of our highways.

It is a mistake to suppose that any novelist can simply lift living persons into his pages. This would be a violation of the technique of his art, and were the same thing as if one pasted a photograph into the middle of a picture. The characters in real fiction have been his own creation, but his imagination has been fed with the material of life. Scott lived among the people of his novels before they took service with him in literature. If he deals very kindly with faithful Caleb Balderstone it was because his own household were so faithful to him. He took a fancy to a poacher that was brought before him for justice and passed him into his own service, and Purdie was his loyal henchman henceforward. When evil days befell Scott and he had to reduce his establishment, Pepe Mathieson, who used to be the coachman, was willing to be the ploughman, and Scott was most grateful for this fealty. " I cannot forget," says Lockhart, " how his eyes sparkled when he first pointed out to me Peter Mathieson guiding the plough on the Haugh. ' Egad,' he said, ' old Pepe and old Pepe's whistling at his darg. The honest fellow said a yoking in a deep field would do baith him and the blackies good.   If things get round with me, easy shall be Pepe's cushion." One of the trials of Scott's life was the death of Thomas Purdie, the ex-poacher and trusty servitor. "I have lost," Scott writes, "my old and faithful servant, and am so much shocked that I really wish to be quit of the country and safe in town.   I have this day laid him in the grave."   This was the inscription on Purdie's tomb —

IN GRATEFUL REMEMBRANCE

OF

THE FAITHFUL

AND ATTACHED SERVICES

OF

TWENTY-TWO YEARS,

AND IN SORROW

FOR THE LOSS OF A HUMBLE

BUT SINCERE FRIEND,

THIS STONE WAS ERECTED

BY

SIR WALTER SCOTT, BART.,

OF ABBOTSFORD.

"Thou hast been faithful
Over a few things,
I will make thee ruler
Over many things."

This is the heart of the *Waverley Novels,* and Scott's sweetest note.

Thomson, the son of the minister of Melrose, who became tutor at Abbotsford, won Scott's heart because he lost his leg in an encounter of his boyhood and refused to betray the name of the companion that had occasioned the mishap. " In the Dominie, like myself, accident has spoiled a capital life-guardsman, and so many were his eccentricities, so rich his learning, and so sound his principles, that he sat for good Dominie Sampson." It may have struck the reader of the *Fair Maid of Perth* that the physical timidity of Conachar, the young Highland chief, and the disgrace of his flight from the battle on the North Inch of Perth, where his henchmen had died so bravely for him, was written with a certain sympathy of feeling. That passage in which one is made to pity the poor lad was Scott's atonement for perhaps the one cruel deed of his life, his contemptuous anger against a brother who had refused to fight a duel (he was willing to fight one in old age himself). A lover of all dumb animals, he pays his tribute to Maida and his other favourite dogs in Bevis, the noble hound of *Woodstock,* and many another friendly fellow, whom his hand touches gently in fiction. When the Baron of Bradwardine comes down to Janet's cottage and Waverley and he have their supper together, Ban and Buscar have also their share. They play their loyal part, too, and Scott is still teaching his lesson of fidelity as much as when he wrote the epitaph on old Maida —

"Beneath the sculptured form, which late you wore,
    Sleep soundly, Maida, at your master's door."

When the Antiquary came forward at the young fisherman's funeral and said that, as landlord to the deceased, he would carry his head to the grave, it was Scott's own heart speaking, and old Alison Breck, among the fish-women, swore almost aloud, funeral though it was. "His honour Monkbarns should never want sax warp of oysters in the season (of which fish he was understood to be fond) if she should gang to sea and dredge for them herself, in the foulest wind that ever blew." It was when staying with a friend at Loch Lomond that he bethought himself of *Rob Roy* and laid out the scenery in his mind, and among his acquaintances he found the de-

lightful Antiquary. The Epic of Jeanie
Deans he took from actual life, and even the
smugglers' secret cellars in *Redgauntlet* he
had found at Berwick. The Covenanters of
a later generation he had seen and not particu-
larly loved, and the old Scots gossips who
talk in the post-office scene — one of the
most successful interiors of Scott — he had
met in many a cottage. He is most convincing when he is dealing with Scots life; young
Waverley, the English squire, is a shadow beside the Antiquary, and Scott himself describes him as a sneaking piece of imbecility,
and declared his conviction that " if he had
married Flora M'Ivor she would have set
him up upon the chimneypiece." The English peasant in Scott's novels is a wooden
figure beside Cuddie Headrigg, and the London cashier a poor ghost in the presence of
Bailie Nicol Jarvie. If his Scots lairds, and
Scots peasants, and Scots women of the working class are not real, and do not carry themselves as flesh and blood, then there is no re-
ality in fiction.

With all his inherent nobility of soul and
personal elevation above everything mean,
Scott had a thorough appreciation of what

has been called, and no word so accurately
describes it, the " pawkiness " of Scots character, which is shared in some degree by all
classes from ploughmen to ecclesiastics, and
of which a Bailie is often the perfect imper-
sonation.   And this characteristic quality of
the Scots people has been immortalised in one
of Scott's most felicitous passages, when Niel
Blane gives directions to his daughter how to
manage the public-house in the trying days
of Claverhouse and the Covenanters. " Jenny,
this is the first day that ye are to take
the place of your worthy mother in attending
to the public; a douce woman she was, civil
to the customers, and had a good name wi'
Whig and Tory, baith up the street and doun
the street.   It will be hard for you to fill
her place, especially on sic a thrang day as
this; but Heaven's will maun be obeyed.
Jenny, whatever Milnwood ca's for, be sure
he maun hae't, for he's the captain o' the
Popinjay, and auld customs maun be supported; if he canna pay the lawing himsell, as
I ken he's keepit unco short by the head, I'll
find a way to shame it out o' his uncle.— The
curate is playing at dice wi' Cornet Grahame.
Be eident and civil to them baith — clergy

and captains can gie an unco deal o' fash in
thae times, where they take an ill-will.— The
dragoons will be crying for ale, and they
wunna want it, and maunna want it — they are
unruly chiels, but they pay ane some gate or
other. I gat the humle-cow, that's the best
in the byre, frae black Frank Inglis and
Sergeant Bothwell for ten pund Scots, and
they drank out the price at ae downsitting.
. . . Whist! ye silly tawpie, we have
naething to do how they come by the bestial
they sell — be that atween them and their
consciences.— Aweel.— Take notice, Jenny,
of that dour, stour-looking carle that sits by
the cheek o' the ingle, and turns his back on
a' men. He looks like one o' the hill folk,
for I saw him start a wee when he saw the
redcoats, and I jalouse he wad hae liked to
hae ridden by, but his horse (it's a good geld-
ing) was ower sair travailed; he behoved to
stop whether he wad or no. Serve him can-
nily, Jenny, and wi' little din, and dinna
bring the sodgers on him by speering ony
questions at him; but let him no hae a room
to himsell, they wad say ye were hiding him.
— For yoursell, Jenny, ye'll be civil to a' the
folk, and take nae heed o' ony nonsense and

daffing the young lads may say t'ye.   Folk in
the hostler line maun put up wi' muckle.
Your mither, rest her saul, could put up wi' as
muckle as maist women — but off hands is
fair play; and if onybody be uncivil ye may
gie me a cry.— Aweel, when the malt begins
to get aboon the meal, they'll begin to speak
about government in kirk and state, and then,
Jenny, they are like to quarrel — let them be
doing — anger's a drouthy passion, and the
mair they dispute, the mair ale they'll drink;
but ye were best serve them wi' a pint o' the
sma' browst, it will heat them less, and they'll
never ken the difference."

Scott's religious position has been, as was
inevitable, the subject of keen controversy, for
Scotland has ever been a land of theological
debate, and is to-day living up with spirit to
her ancient character.   When Sir Walter
opened the novel of *Old Mortality* on the 5th
of May 1679, and plunged into the life of that
day in the West of Scotland, he took his courage in both his hands, for he chose the period
and the scene of the hottest conflict in Scots
history.   Owing partly to the wildness of the
scenery and partly to the intensity of the people, the history of Scotland has been one long

romance, and from the Reformation, religion was the original cause and burning fire of every controversy. No one can understand Scots history without fixing in his mind that religion has played the chief part in the making of Scots life, and that the Scots have been ready to argue and to fight, not only about the great principles which have divided, say the Roman from the Protestant faith, but also about the jots and tittles of their creed. Fine scruples have created parties within the Scots Kirk which are almost innumerable, and which certainly are now unintelligible to the modern mind. Sir Walter has crystallised the *perfervidum ingenium* of the Scots folk in this book, and staged not the politics only but the theology of Scotland. There were the Cavaliers under Claverhouse hunting the Presbyterians, who were hiding on the moors, and meeting in Conventicles for worship, and the Covenanters growing ever more bitter and determined under this persecution, till at last they were ready to renounce allegiance to the King, as well as to denounce the Bishops, and there were the less extreme Presbyterians who thought that their brethren had gone too far, and endeavoured to reconcile their own religious principles with loyalty to government. This was the situation of *Old Mortality,* and these the feelings which moved its characters. Scott's insight and fairness must be judged by his studies of Claverhouse on the one hand, and the Presbyterian ministers on the other, and it has been difficult to satisfy every person about Claverhouse. Macaulay, who is neither a Covenanter nor an advocate of their particular case, asserts that Claverhouse goaded the peasantry of the Western Lowlands into madness, and murdered a pious Covenanter called Brown before his wife's eyes, while in Napier's *Memoirs of Dundee* Grahame is represented as a patriotic Scotsman as well as a gallant soldier, and this was also the portrait drawn by another Jacobite man of letters, Charles Kirkpatrick Sharpe. " Bloody Claverhouse " was the Covenanting nickname, and " Bonnie Dundee " was the Cavalier description of the same man, and it is only less dangerous to hold the scales of justice in the life of Claverhouse than in that of Queen Mary. It was to his credit that he was on bad terms with the drunken politicians of the day, and that he remained to the end of his career an unselfish loyalist, doing all that

in him lay for the Stuart family, with very
little thanks from either them or their ad-
visers, and that he died at the battle of Kil-
liecrankie fighting for a lost cause. It was
not the least of his exploits that he won
the heart of Lady Jean Cochrane, whose
mother was an extreme Covenanter; but there
seems little doubt that behind a fair face and
graceful manner he hid a determined and un-
swerving purpose, that to his friends he was
tender and true, and to the enemies of his
cause absolutely murderous, and that in spite
of the apologies of his biographer, Napier,
and the glamour cast round him in *Lays of the
Scottish Cavaliers,* he treated the Covenanters
with great cruelty and did not shrink from
military murders. Upon the whole I am inclined to think that the study of Grahame in
Old Mortality, although it has been so severely criticised in Covenanting quarters, is
not far from the truth, for full justice is done
to his personal attractiveness and disinterested
loyalty, while his disregard of popular rights
and his indifference to suffering are clearly
represented.

Whether Scott has rendered equal justice to
the other side is another question, and per-

haps he ought not to have prejudiced the case
by caricaturing the names of the Covenanting
ministers. One is inclined beforehand to laugh
at clergymen who are called Poundtext or Kettledrummle, or Habakkuk Mucklewrath.
The reader must, however, remember that the
names are only the license of a novelist, and
that the Presbyterian minister did not pound
his text any more clumsily, and that he was
not any more a kettledrum in the matter of
noise than the Episcopalian curate of the day.
One cannot tell who sat for Poundtext, but
for Kettledrummle and Mucklewrath one sus-
pects that Scott depended upon the lives of
Peden and Cameron, as told with remarkable
felicity of style by Patrick Walker, in the
book called *Biographia Presbyteriana*. Patrick Walker could tell a story with engaging
vigour, and was a great favourite with Robert Louis Stevenson, who, in his *Letters,* vol. ii.
p. 312, says: " I have lately been returning to
my wallowing in the mire. When I was a
child, and indeed until I was nearly a man, I
consistently read Covenanting books. Now
that I am a grey-beard — or would be if I
could raise the beard — I have returned, and
for weeks back have read little else but Wod-

row, Walker, Shields, &c." McBriar, whom Scott treats with more respect, is almost certainly Hugh McKail, a young clergyman of delicate constitution and beautiful character, who threw himself into the Covenanting cause, and was involved in the " Pentland Rising." He was taken prisoner and put to death in Edinburgh in the twenty-sixth year of his age. During his trial he was tortured in the " boots," and Scott has used the scene in *Old Mortality*. McKail was a high-spirited enthusiast, and his last words on the scaffold were: " I ascend to my Father and your Father, to my God and your God — to my King and your King, to the blessed Apostles and Martyrs, and to the city of the living God, the Heavenly Jerusalem, to an innumerable company of Angels, to the general assembly of the first-born, to God the Judge of all, to the spirits of just men made perfect, and to Jesus the mediator of the new covenant; and I bid you all farewell, for God will be more comfortable to you than I could be, and He will be now more refreshing to me than you could be. Farewell, farewell in the Lord! "

From the moderate Presbyterian clergy, so

poorly represented by Poundtext, Scott might have taken men like Robert Douglas, of whom it was written: " He was a great state preacher, one of the greatest of that age in Scotland, for he feared no man to declare the mind of God to him, yet very accessible and easy to be conversed with." Or Lawrence Charteris, who was described by Bishop Burnet as " a perfect friend and a most sublime Christian. He did not talk of the defects of his kind like an angry reformer, but like a man full of a deep but humble sense of them." He used to say the defection among them has been " from the temper and conversation which the Gospel requires of us."   Above all he could have chosen Leighton, who was first of all a Presbyterian minister and then a Bishop, but above all a Christian; and Carstairs, who was persecuted before the Reformation, and after the Reformation became the most powerful man in Scotland, who showed the greatest kindness to the party that had persecuted him, and was beyond question the ablest clergyman of his day. It is always a misfortune, and one may find a contemporary illustration, when any body of men are driven into extreme views and desperate actions, for they become either absurd or fanatical, and

the real conscience and courage of the Covenanters have been much disfigured by a want
of charity in their utterances and common
sense in their policy. But it is well to remember that they were not all Kettle-
drummles, and Scott declares in a note to *Old
Mortality,* that if he had to rewrite the tale
he would give the Moderate Party a better
representative than Peter Poundtext, and even
the severest critic of Scott from the Covenanting side must admit that in Jeanie Deans
he drew a perfect type of humble Scots
piety.

Is it wonderful that the extreme wing of
Scots religion, which has not always been in
profound sympathy with literature, has found
some difficulty in accepting Scott as an
interpreter of our nation, when Thomas Carlyle, who was by instinct a man of letters, has
not dealt so generously with his distinguished
fellow-countryman as those who love both
men could desire. Among certain admirable
doctrines of the Roman faith there is one
called " invincible ignorance " which ought to
be allowed greater play in every controversy,
theological or political, and not least in racial
misunderstandings. By our heredity and environment, by the books we have read and the

men who have taught us, by the blood in our
veins and the people among whom we have
lived, we are apt to be so impressed and so
biassed as to be blinded to the truth of a creed
which is not ours, and the excellence of men
who are of another type. It were a counsel
of perfection to ask from a Puritan justice to
Charles I. and Oliver Cromwell, and although it was a fine achievement of Erasmus
to appreciate at their value both Luther and
Pope Leo X., that humanist is a rare figure
in history, and I am sorry to say not a force
in affairs. People full of the strong wine of
Scots controversy are apt to speak as if there
has been only one Scotland; the Scotland created by John Knox and the ministers of the
Kirk, by the theology of Calvin and the democratic education of the parish school, and represented admirably and successfully by that
middle class which has supplied the elders to
the Kirk and the traders to foreign parts, and
up to this time has made Scotland intelligent
and prosperous. They forget that there has
been always another Scotland since the days
of Queen Mary, of Catholics, Episcopalians,
Jacobites, and Moderate Kirkmen, like that
excellent man of sincerity and courtesy, who

ended a note to John Knox, " Farewell in
Christ, and endeavour to let truth prevail and
not the man," and Archbishop Leighton who
was weary of wrangling, and Carstairs who
held the scales level between both sides, and
the literary men who, at the close of the
eighteenth century, made Edinburgh glorious
through the world. Unto this Scotland belonged for the most part the soldiers, the great
lawyers, poets, and scholars, and of this line
Scott had come. He was a Cavalier whose
heart was with Prince Charles, though his
reason was with King George, who could appreciate the courage of the Covenanters, but
whose own attitude would have been that of
Young Morton in *Old Mortality*. Scott in
his geniality and charity, his sympathies with
the virtues of a chivalrous past, and his in-
stinctive dislike of religious extremity, was a
Moderate, and has behind him a minority,
perhaps, of the Scots people, but a minority
commanding respect for its appreciation of a
storied past, its devotion to Art and Letters,
its love of peace and its principle of charity.
It is to the credit of Sir Walter that he, the
descendant of those border raiders, has been
as comprehensive and as tolerant.

Carlyle, on the other hand, whatever may have been his former creed or his local surroundings, was all his days a Calvinist and a democrat, with the narrowness and sincerity, the strength and intolerance of the peasant class from which he sprung. It is natural for Carlyle to ridicule Sir Walter's desire to establish a county family, and one recognises that the ambitions of Abbotsford and Ecclefechan were hopelessly at variance, but as one who received his first literary inspiration from Carlyle's address to the students of Edinburgh University, and who has felt the iron of Carlyle's virile gospel pass as a tonic into his blood, I cannot but regret that Carlyle in his well-known essay did such poor justice to Scott and the *Waverley Novels*. When he speaks of him as writing daily "with the ardour of a steam-engine, that he might make fifteen thousand a year and buy upholstery with it," and pronounces that "his work is not profitable for doctrine or reproof or edification or building up or elevating in any shape," one knows that he has seen Scott in a glass darkly, and that because he had not come with open face. When he enlarges upon Scott as one of the healthiest of men, and allows with condescension that amusement in the way of reading can go no further than his tales, one wishes that Carlyle had left Scott alone and confined himself to Burns, whom he understood from the heart out, for they were by heredity of the same breed. Compare Lockhart's *Scott;* one of the most wholesome biographies in our literature, and the *Life of Carlyle.* Carlyle complains that Scott's biography had run to seven volumes, but his in one shape or other has run to several volumes more, and no one can be sure when it will be finally concluded, and his grave be left in peace. Carlyle is in serious doubt whether Scott was a great man, and while he admits he was a demigod among the circulating heroes of the library, he sees no likelihood of a place for him among the great writers of all ages. Well, the books stand together upon the shelf of every student of literature and Scots history; we can form our own judgment of greatness. It is a means of grace to read Scott's life, in which, if nothing is set down in malice, nothing is extenuated, for his stainless purity in which there was no touch of austerity, his winsome good nature which never seemed to fail, his kindliness to every person and creature that came into contact with him, his too generous help to second-rate writers and rash publishers, his generous forgiveness of the wrongs which he suffered in business affairs, his heroic endurance of the cruellest pain, his early romantic attachment which was the shadow on his life, his chivalrous service of his wife who was not his real love, his courage in the great crash of his affairs, his persistent toil to pay other men's debts, and his gentle, believing death, bring us into an atmosphere in which it is good to live. No woman had ever cause to complain of Scott's rudeness, no man heard him whine about his illnesses, no fellow-writer was contemptuously treated by him, no man was afraid to speak to him. He had no affectations, either in style or manner; he had neither grudges nor jealousies; every one loved him — his wife, his children, his friends, his printers, his servants, his dogs. " Scott," says Lord Tennyson, " is the most chivalrous literary figure of this century, and the author with the finest range since Shakespeare." His was the greatness of faith and charity, and one may hold with reason that Scotland has never produced a finer instance of practical and persuasive religion.

The subtle quality of a man's character passes into his work and becomes its preserving salt, but a great writer must submit his work to the arbitrament, not of the popularity of his day, but of the criticism which is above every day. There are books which catch the ear of the people and pass away having served their purpose, there are books which remain and they are the classics. "The last discovery of modern culture," a competent writer says, " is that Scott's prose is commonplace. The young men at our universities are too critical to care for his artless sentences and flowing descriptions. As boys love lollipops, so these juvenile fops love to roll phrases under the tongue, as if phrases in themselves had any value apart from thoughts, feelings, great conceptions of human sympathy." From the circulars of publishers I learn that new editions of Scott are ever appearing, but from private observation I do not find the younger generation is reading Scott, and without any disrespect to the literary craftsmen of the day, this seems to me a calamity. It reminds me of Ruskin's saying, about wondering, not how

much people suffer, but how much they lose.
It may be that Scott has indulged too much in
introductions, and has dared to add notes
which are full of instruction, but which, on
that account, this generation does not desire.
Or it may be that he has not the trick of sen-
sational plot, and did not strike upon the in-
vention of the detective story.   There is, however, good ground for believing that his hold
is permanent, and that in the end his vogue
will be universal.   When estimating Scott we
must remind ourselves what he essayed to do,
and his was that which is the first and will be
the last form of literature.   When the first
half-dozen humans gathered in a cave one
told how he had killed some monstrous beast,
and that was the beginning of letters; when the
last half-dozen huddle together on the cold
earth some one will tell of his battle with a
seal, and that will be the end of letters.   Literature began with a story, and nothing so holds
the human mind, and the genius of Sir Walter Scott was the genius of the story.   Let us
grant that his style was not " precious," let us
even grant that it was sometimes redundant, if
you please slipshod, he could afford even if he
chose to be ungrammatical.   His was the easy

undress of one whose position was assured and who was indifferent to little conventionalities. Between the books of precocious moderns and the *Waverley Novels* there is the same difference as between the trim lawn and the neat little beds of a villa garden, and the mountain side with the swelling waves of purple heather and the emerald green between. It partakes of a debating society to inquire which is his greatest book, but I suppose his mightiest three are *Old Mortality,* the *Antiquary,* and the *Heart of Midlothian.* With those three and his Shakespeare a man might be content. For this is the large and wealthy place of literature, where you breathe the air of Homer and of Virgil, of Dante and Milton. And for a single passage of passion and pathos I can only remember one other from Thackeray to be compared with the plea which Jeanie Deans made with the Queen for her sister's life:—

"O, madam, if ever ye kend what it was to sorrow for and with a sinning and a suffering creature, whose mind is sae tossed that she can be neither ca'd fit to live or die, have some compassion on our misery! Save an honest house from dishonour, and an unhappy

girl, not eighteen years of age, from an early
and dreadful death! Alas! it is not when
we sleep soft and wake merrily ourselves that
we think on other people's sufferings. Our
hearts are waxed light within us then, and we
are for righting our ain wrangs and fighting
our ain battles. But when the hour of trouble
comes to the mind or to the body — and seldom may it visit your leddyship — and when
the hour of death comes, that comes to high
and low — lang and late may it be yours —
O, my leddy, then it isna what we hae dune
for oursels, but what we hae dune for others,
that we think on maist pleasantly. And the
thought that ye hae intervened to spare the
puir thing's life will be sweeter in that hour,
come when it may, than if a word of your
mouth could hang the haill Porteous mob at
the tail of ae tow." [1]

And yet, and I quote a modern: " This
glorious poet, without whom our very conception of human development would have
ever been imperfect, this manliest and truest
and widest of romances, we neglect for some
hothouse hybrid of psychological analysis, for
the wretched imitators of Balzac and the

[1] *Heart of Midlothian*, vol. ii. chap. xii. p. 210.

jackanapes phrasemongering of some Osric of our day, who assure us that Scott is an " absolute Philistine." It remains, however, that a man may be greater than his work. If there be any goodness throughout the *Waverley Novels,* it was the inspiration of their writer. They have added to the company of our friends many high-spirited women and many gallant gentlemen, they have taught us to think more kindly of human nature and to seek after the highest things, but they have introduced us to no braver or truer man than Scott himself. Unintoxicated by prosperity and unbroken in adversity, toiling to redeem that dreadful debt while his wife lay dying, and after her death going back to his work without any public moan, he did his part right knightly. With Shakespeare he is the chief creative genius of our English literature, and with Burns he is the proud glory of Scots letters. And now, if in jealous affection we have complained that Carlyle did less than justice to Scott's work, we gladly accept his beautiful tribute to Scott's character. " When he departed he took a man's life along with him. No sounder piece of British manhood was put together in that eighteenth century of time. Alas, his fine Scotch face, with its shaggy honesty, sagacity, and goodness, when we saw it latterly on the Edinburgh streets, was all worn with care, the joy all fled from it: ploughed deep with labour and sorrow. We shall never forget it; we shall never see it again.   Adieu, Sir Walter, pride of all Scotsmen, take our proud and sad farewell."

THE END